ROBERT LOUIS STEVENSON

ROBERT LOUIS STEVENSON

by

LETTICE COOPER

" Character, character is what he has !"
HENRY JAMES

London

HOME & VAN THAL LTD.

First published 1947
Reprinted 1949

PRINTED IN GREAT BRITAIN BY
MORRISON AND GIBB LTD., LONDON AND EDINBURGH
FOR HOME AND VAN THAL LTD., 36 GREAT RUSSELL STREET, LONDON, W.C.I

CONTENTS

CHAPTER I

THE CHILD

ROBERT LOUIS STEVENSON was born in Edinburgh on the 13th of November 1850. His inheritance was distinguished; the Stevenson family were brilliant engineers with an international reputation. His grandfather, Robert Stevenson, was Engineer to the Board of Northern Lights, and had built the Bell Rock Lighthouse. His father, Thomas Stevenson, had constructed most of the lighthouses on the western coast and islands of Scotland. They were both architects and builders; the plans which they articulated in Edinburgh they carried out with much hardship and some danger in places where no man had built before, on ledges of rock and spurs of island under the howling assault of the Atlantic. Thomas Stevenson, especially, was a man of inventive genius. He made many improvements to the apparatus used in lighthouses and perfected the machinery for revolving lights. He was not a trained scientist, he worked by intuition with the spring of the creative artist. He had a particular gift for seeing the way to overcome difficulties which seemed insuperable. His work was a vocation to him and he was justly proud of his achievements. His firm were consulting engineers to the Governments of India, New Zealand and Japan. Thomas Stevenson was deeply romantic and loved every detail of the struggle against wind and water for the lives of men. To this inheritance, creative energy, constructive work of great delicacy and precision and a persevering courage, the child, Robert Louis, was born.

9

The other chief part of his inheritance was religion. Thomas Stevenson had, so his son wrote, " a clansman's loyalty to the Church of Scotland." An austere morality was his ruling passion. He was melancholy by nature in spite of a genial public manner, and Louis speaks of his father's " sense of the fleetingness of life, and of his concern for death." He married Margaret Balfour, youngest daughter and thirteenth child of the minister of Colinton. Her great-great-grandfather was the famous Whig lawyer, James Balfour, her family tree was thick with lawyers and divines, and she was related to the border Elliots and through them distantly to Sir Walter Scott. In her, too, piety was the mainspring, but it was a less sombre piety than her husband's. She was gentle, gay, graceful, charming. She had an early delicacy of the lungs which she outgrew, but which she handed on to her only child.

He was even more alone than most only children. In the summer there were visits to Colinton and the entrancing company of his cousins, the swarming brood of Balfour children. In the bleak Edinburgh winter he was often ill with chest complaints and sometimes had to be kept indoors for weeks at a time. So restricted and bearing the full pressure of family concern and family feelings, it was inevitable that he should escape early into fantasy, nor did he have to find his own way there. There was an unexpected boyish streak in Thomas Stevenson. The responsible engineer and severe moralist put himself to sleep every night of his life by telling himself stories about " ships, roadside inns, robbers, old sailors and commercial travellers before the era of steam." No doubt he told some of these tales to the child when he lay in bed, feverish with bronchitis and with terror of " the jet black night, that stares through the window pane." Louis' imagination was nourished, too, by his nurse, Alison Cunningham. She had, her nursling says, a natural pleasure in words. " She read the work of others as a poet would hardly dare to read his own, gloating over the rhythm, dwelling with delight on the assonances and the alliterations." She recited hymns and metrical psalms, and for hours at a time she read him Bible stories and stories of the sufferings of the Covenanters, whose sombre tradition set the key for the household. " I spent," he says, " a Covenanting childhood." Like so many other English writers, Stevenson had the language and rhythm of the Bible as the foundation of his craft.

He began early to practise it. First with a toy theatre. He tells us in his essay, *A Penny Plain and Twopence Coloured*, that it was not only the sight in a Leith Walk shop window of a theatre in working order with " a forest set " or " combat " or " robbers carousing " that enchanted him. " Below and about, dearer tenfold to me, the plays themselves, those budgets of romance tumbled one upon another. Every sheet we fingered was another lightning glance into obscure, delicious story : it was like wallowing in the raw stuff of story books." Soon it was not enough for him to wallow, he must begin to imitate and write. His lazy and intermittent attendances at school were no more than interruptions to the self-education that he has described in one of his best-known passages.

" I was always busy upon my private end, which was to learn to write. I kept always two books in my pocket, one to read, one to write in. As I walked my mind was busy fitting what I saw with appropriate words. . . . Thus I lived with words. Whenever I read a book or a passage that particularly pleased me. . . . I must sit down at once and set myself to ape that quality. I have thus played the sedulous ape to Hazlitt, to Lamb, to Wordsworth, to Sir Thomas Browne, to Defoe, to Hawthorne, to Montaigne, and to Baudelaire, to Obermann."

He was fifteen when his first book, a short account of the Pentland Rising of 1666, an unsuccessful revolt of the Covenanters against their persecutors, was published anonymously by an Edinburgh bookseller. It opened with the high solemnity appropriate to his years. " Two hundred years ago a tragedy was enacted in Scotland the memory of which has been in great measure lost or obscured by the deep tragedies which followed. It is, as it were, the evening of the night of persecution." Thomas Stevenson, who had financed the early venture, bought up all the unsold copies, and the pamphlet is now a rare collector's piece. To the father, this writing was a hobby enforced on the delicate boy by his inability for rougher sports. He had as yet no idea that it was not an engineer he was rearing. Nor did he realise, when he sent Louis and his mother for recuperative holidays to Mentone, that he was giving his son a first taste of another world, a world of warmer seas and hot sunshine, of flowers and wine and easier living, a world for which he was always to be a little homesick in the windy streets of Edinburgh, just as in Samoa his heart was to turn back with longing to his grey Northern birthplace. He was never happy or well in Edinburgh, but the city gave him, if nothing else, a sense of history. It was not without effect that his walks with his nurse and his schoolboy wanderings led him through streets where the past is alive in every stone.

The indifferent schoolboy passed into Edinburgh University and became an idle undergraduate. He was supposed to be reading for a degree in science and engineering, but he seldom attended the lectures. All his energy went into his secret apprenticeship to his life's passion. To the outward eye he drifted unsatisfactorily, interested only when talking. Already his personality was notable to strangers. Mrs. Fleeming Jenkin, wife of his Professor, spoke of her first meeting with "the young Heine with a Scotch accent who spoke as Charles Lamb wrote." During his vacation his father sent him to the harbour works on the coasts of Fife and Caithness to get a foretaste of the practical side of his supposed career. He enjoyed this holiday, if not in the way he was meant to He spent his time looking, and choosing words to describe what he saw. On this visit he began the habit of letter writing which was to last to his life's end, and to give so vivid a picture of the craftsman engaged in his craft. From Anstruther and Wick he wrote to his mother, with whom his relationship was always easier than with his father, about himself and other people and the sea. It does not appear that he gave more than the overflow of his attention to engineering.

The family crisis was approaching. When he was twenty Louis broke it to his father that he did not mean to be an engineer but to earn his living as a writer. The blow was considerable. The boy's rejection seemed to belittle all the honourable work and tradition which were the pride of Thomas Stevenson's life. There had, however, always been a doubt as to whether Louis would be strong enough for lighthouse building, and his father reluctantly accepted his refusal. The alternative he would not accept. Writing was an uncertain, not a creditable profession for a gentleman, there was no future in it. Louis must read law if he would not go on with engineering. Then he would be called to the Bar and find a respectable outlet for his craze for using words.

Louis did read law with no more application than he had read engineering. His mood was half defiant, half ashamed. He began to dress like an artist and to go about with low company, partly because he found there an ease and freedom from restraint which he missed in his father's circle. With his long hair and casual, untidy clothes, " Velvet Coat " sat in the sanded kitchen of a shady public-house, " the companion of seamen, chimney sweeps and thieves, my circle constantly changed by the action of the police magistrate." What a Villon the young sinner felt himself to be as he sat there in the dubious pub making notes—for he had not abandoned one inch of his purpose—in a penny notebook !

It was bad enough to his family that he should go, and be known to go, to such places, but worse still that he met women there. Early biographers carefully ignored this side of the boy's initiation, but Henley, writing of the " lover and sensualist," knew better. It was probably not a happy beginning, the affairs were tinged with the discomfort of the Puritan let loose. Louis was romantic, and somewhere in this underworld of Edinburgh he fell in love and proposed to take the girl out of her brothel and marry her, but he had no money, and his appalled parents were naturally not willing to finance such a marriage. He must really have known this perfectly well, and it is impossible to say how deep the thing went, or how far it was only a gesture of defiance.

There was another shock in store for Thomas Stevenson, worse than the desertion of the engineer, or the antics of the nascent Bohemian. With the full dramatic value only possible in such a household, Louis lost his faith. He wrote to his friend Charles Baxter, who throughout his life played a faithful Horatio to his Hamlet, " On Friday night my father put me one or two questions as to beliefs which I candidly answered." These candid answers sent both parents to bed ill, and made Louis feel that he was playing a part in a tragedy, not, perhaps, without a certain relish. He was always deeply interested in his own development. " I am not, as they call me, a careless infidel. I believe as much as they do, only generally in the inverse ratio." He adds with the solemnity of his twenty-two years, " I have not come hastily to my views. O Lord, what a pleasant thing it is to have just damned the happiness of probably the only two people who care a damn about you in the world."

For the moment home was no more home to him. Disapproval, guilt, the bitter cold of the Edinburgh climate, and the exhausting sense of being cramped at every turn were making him really ill. He went to pay a visit to friends in a rectory in the South of England, and there made a friendship that was to help to change the world for him. Mrs. Sitwell was staying in the rectory and was joined there by Sidney Colvin, whom she was soon to marry. He was at this time twenty-nine years old and Slade Professor of the Fine Arts, later to be Keeper of Prints at the British Museum. He became from that visit Louis' guide, comfort and support, his lifelong friend. They sent Stevenson to a London specialist, who at once ordered him to the South of France. What Mrs. Sitwell and Colvin did for him was to recognise the quality of his talent and to accept as perfectly reasonable his ambition to become a writer. It was the confirmation from outside that he needed, and in that year he first produced work which was published. From now onwards the story is the story of the writer.

So at twenty-two, there he is . . . thin to emaciation, with very bright brown eyes, light hair worn long, deliberately careless clothes, and an airy, nervous manner ; an over-disciplined, over-indulged, lonely young man, tied to his parents by every string of his heart, yet impelled by his urgent vitality to make his own life apart from them ; conscious of failure and disgrace in their eyes, yet aware of other standards ; aching for congenial company and congenial achievement ; lazy, industrious, shy, talkative, generous, egotistical ; in the eyes of his father's circle in Edinburgh a shocking misfortune for the Stevensons ; to the Colvins a youth of infinite promise, worth any trouble and already much loved. There he is, handicapped for life by congenital delicacy, but equipped with a high spirit : apparently desultory, giving the impression of a lightweight ; not easily perceived to be a strenuous young man with a deep-rooted purpose on which he has already been working for at least a dozen years.

CHAPTER II

APPRENTICESHIP

THE young writer walked on to a stage that was still crowded although some of the stars had vanished. Thackeray had died ten years before, Dickens three years, but George Eliot had just published *Middlemarch,* and had yet to publish *Daniel Deronda* ; Meredith was in mid-career, Hardy had written three novels. The chorus of poets included Tennyson, Matthew Arnold, Browning, Christina Rossetti, Swinburne. John Stuart Mill died in that year. Darwin, whose *Origin of Species* was now thirteen years old, had just published the *Descent of Man.* Carlyle was writing, William Morris and Ruskin. The age teemed with writers and the writers wrote abundantly. The novelists especially drew upon a wealth of invention unsurpassed by any group except the great Russians. The form of the novel did not interest them. With lavish carelessness they poured their riches into sacks that bulged to shapelessness with their plenty. Selection was not one of their virtues. Romance, realism, extravagance, experience, fantasy, observation, everything went into the Christmas pudding of the mid-Victorian novel.

Stevenson, who had grown up preoccupied with the choice of words, whose talent was smaller and more clearly defined, was already breaking away from this tradition, though he was not yet ready to write novels. His first published works were essays, remarkable at once for a certain distinction of style, but suggesting that the young writer had as yet more wish to write than anything to say. *Roads*, the first of his work to be accepted, was published in the *Portfolio*. It is an account of impressions gathered while he was walking in Suffolk. His second essay, *Ordered South*, which appeared in *Macmillan's Magazine*, gives a picture of himself at that time, a very sick and sorry young man alone on the French Riviera in that state of nervous exhaustion in which he sees the natural beauties of his beloved Mediterranean coast with " a cold head knowledge of beauty " " divorced from enjoyment." He was half dead from the protracted family struggle, but being a writer in grain managed to make something even of that sensation. He wrote rather grandly of his willingness to die. Later, when he reprinted his early essay, he recanted this literary resignation. It would be a mistake to think of him, even at this stage of his life, as a depressing figure. Few young men are as melancholy as their writings, and by the time Colvin came out to join him he was already shaking off the mood of *Ordered South* as he recovered his strength and began to find congenial company. The impression that he made upon his friends then and at all times was one of a stimulating vitality. They never saw him nor heard from him without feeling that his vivid interest in life and in writing quickened theirs. " You seem to me," Edmund Gosse wrote to him, " the personification of life," and though Colvin in those years did so much to advise and help, he valued the friendship from the beginning no more for Stevenson's sake than for his own.

When Stevenson came back to Edinburgh in the next summer he was in much better health and spirits, cheered by the knowledge that he had made a beginning, if a small one, in his chosen profession, and had sympathetic friends who believed in him as a writer. His life was no longer bounded by his home, but he was still torn by the difficult relationship with his father. Somehow he managed to pass his final examination in law at Edinburgh University, and was admitted to the Scottish Bar. In a desperate attempt to please his father, he even walked the hall of Parliament House for a month waiting for work, but it could only be a form. His real work was waiting for him, and this was his last attempt to comply with his father's ideas of how he should live. He gave up all pretence of trying to be a lawyer, and spent the next year or two moving about between Scotland, London, where he stayed with the Colvins and other friends, and France.

Here, with his cousin Bob Stevenson, in the Latin Quarter of Paris or in the artist colony at Barbizon, in the Forest of Fontainebleau, he was happiest of all. He loved French writers, French people and French ways of living. "Wherever I meet a Frenchman," he said later, "I am at home." After the strict Edinburgh household, the happy-go-lucky ways of the artist community were a glorious release. Bob Stevenson was as fond of talking about everything under the sun as he was. Here was no moral censorship to live up to, no embargo on free discussion, but easy ways and casual clothes, plenty of cheap wine which he loved, and the companionship of people concentrating like himself on the technical problems of their art. The open-air life of the forest suited his health and he was the liveliest in the group of young men who waited eagerly for his reappearances.

He was always writing, but as a writer before the public he made slow progress ; *Roads* was published in 1873. In the next year he had four articles printed in different magazines, including *Ordered South* and *Victor Hugo's Romances*, an article which he remarked was the first in which he found himself able to say things in the way in which he felt they should be said. It was published in the *Cornhill* by Leslie Stephen, who at once recognised Stevenson's promise, encouraged him and gave him introductions in the literary world, among others to Henley, soon to become one of his greatest friends.

In 1875 Stevenson had only two essays accepted, *Autumn Effects* and *Knox*. Thomas Stevenson must have thought that he had been right in saying that it was not easy for an author to live by his profession, and there were times when Stevenson was deeply troubled at taking so much help from his father, but he had his share of the necessary egotism of the artist. In spite of his small output his reputation was growing. *A Lodging for the Night*, his first short story to be accepted, was published in 1877. It is a story about Villon, with whom as a young man he evidently identified himself. It opens brilliantly with a murder in a tavern, and with Villon wandering through the streets of Paris on a wintry night looking for shelter or for someone to rob, but the end, when he finds the old man alone in his house and is entertained by him, has less certainty of touch as though Stevenson was not really sure what point the story was making. It shows what he himself said later was the distinguishing mark of his fiction, " the exact description of physical states," for the reader feels with Villon the bitter cold of the Paris streets and the chill of his sopping clothes.

In the next year Stevenson published his first book, *An Inland Voyage*. It was the account of a journey made by canoe from Antwerp up the Scheldt and the Belgian Canals to the upper waters of the Oise. Stevenson himself described the book, which was written up afterwards from a log made at the time, as "not badly written, thin, mildly cheery and strained." Strain often is and always should be more apparent to the writer than to the reader. The book is slight, but it reads easily. It has the charm of a leisurely holiday, a pleasantly observant note, and the distinction of style which had already made a small circle look eagerly for the appearance of the initials R.L.S. in the *Cornhill*. Outside this small circle neither the *Inland Voyage* nor the book which followed it, *Travels with a Donkey in the Cevennes*, made much impression. Stevenson was still a promising young writer from whom his discerning friends hoped for much, but of whom the reading world in general were unaware. He was still dependent on his father for most of his livelihood.

He was coming to a crisis in his life at which it was to become an urgent question whether he could keep himself and not only himself. There are hints in the *Inland Voyage* that the days of irresponsibility are nearly over. "You may paddle all day long, but it is when you come back at nightfall and look in at the familiar room that you find Love and Death waiting for you beside the stove, and the most beautiful adventures are not those you seek." Stevenson's most beautiful adventure had already found him.

The artist community in the forest at Grez did not include women. It was an American woman, used to the greater freedom of the new world, who first gate-crashed the monastic circle because she wished to paint.

Stevenson heard of the intrusion in Paris, and was amused, mock-indignant and curious. On a warm night he arrived at the inn in the forest, looked through the open window, and saw Fanny Van de Grift Osbourne, with her son and daughter, sitting at the table in the lamplight.   As he looked, he said to Bob Stevenson that he was going to marry her.

It seemed wildly improbable that this could be more than a dream.   Stevenson was twenty-five.   Fanny Osbourne was thirty-six, with a husband in America, a daughter, Belle, only eight years younger than Stevenson, and a son, Lloyd Osbourne, eight years old.   Her husband was unfaithful and they did not get on, but there was no idea of a permanent separation.   She had come to France for a rest and for education for her children, and was mourning at that time the death of her youngest child in Paris.   Even if she had been free neither she nor Stevenson had any money.   The romance looked as unpromising as possible, but the suitor had no doubts about the end.   Stevenson always knew what he wanted and went after it with persevering energy.   " I am consistent in my schemes," he once said.   With the same determination with which he had trained himself from childhood to write, he now set himself to marry Fanny Osbourne.   Later on he put twenty-five as the age when his youth ended.

The new experience released new feeling in his work.   In *Falling in Love*, one of the essays written at this time, and later published in *Virginibus Puerisque*, he speaks of the man who " now has to deal with commanding emotions instead of with the easy dislikes and preferences in which he has hitherto passed his days."   Of " falling at once into a state in which another person becomes the very gist and centre of God's creation, and demolishes our laborious theories with a smile."   " The love of life itself is translated into a wish to remain in the same world with so precious and desirable a fellow creature."

In the same world, but not for the time being in the same

continent. After two years in France made happy by constant visits from Louis, Fanny Osbourne went back to America. She at least believed that the parting was final : she was held back by " the interests and feelings of others " from trying for a divorce, but the attempt to live with her husband again was a complete failure, and she decided to give it up. She applied for a divorce. The news came to Stevenson, and with it news that she was ill and miserable. He at once determined to go to her. He told his parents, to whom it seemed his worst folly yet. Louis, not established in any profession, to rush off to America, to marry a divorcée eleven years older than himself ! Louis, who could not earn his own living, to take on a wife and two stepchildren ! His father would have nothing to do with it. There would be no help with the journey, no supplies from home. He was not deterred. With what money he had he took a passage on an emigrant ship, the only one he could afford. He was not without a certain satisfaction in his own dramatic decision. " No man is any use until he has dared everything," he wrote to Colvin. " I feel just now as if I had, so might become a man." In this spirit he set out on the venture which was to wreck his health, shorten his life, but assure a great deal of his happiness.

CHAPTER III

"THE AMATEUR EMIGRANT"

THE voyage was trying. Scanty food, discomforts and anxiety about Fanny made him ill, but he worked, as he wrote to Colvin, like a horse, kept notes all the time for *The Amateur Emigrant*, and nearly finished *The Story of a Lie*, which he wrote "in a slantindicular cabin with the table playing bob-cherry with the ink bottle." It is a long short story with a weak end, the fault of so much of his work. He often lacked the emotional pressure to carry his design through to its climax. *The Story of a Lie* reflects much of Stevenson. The relationship between father and son is like that of two lovers, they quarrel and suffer with intensity and make friends again in a passion of relief. No doubt the split with his home was not the least of Stevenson's troubles. Another voice of his speaks in the story, for the blustering, prosperous, respectable squire is defeated in the end by the wastrel, sponging vagabond, the careless parent and indifferent painter who yet speaks, not without his own dignity, for a freer and wider world. *The Story of a Lie* was published in the *New Quarterly Magazine* two months after Stevenson landed in New York.

He had a day in New York before the emigrant train started. He tramped from editor to editor in driving rain trying to find an opening for his work. He was turned down everywhere. The initials R. L. S. meant nothing outside the *Cornhill* circle. Later, when America was to claim him as her own discovery, and editors queued up for a contribution from his pen, some of them may have remembered regretfully the untidy young writer, in a dripping mackintosh, whom they sent empty away. Next day he took the train to San Francisco. The journey, which was extremely uncomfortable, took eleven days, and nearly finished him. " What it is to be ill on an emigrant train let those declare who know," he wrote to Henley. He was still interested in his fellow passengers : he noted all the time that Americans were " so very rude and yet so very kind "— and he was still making notes for *The Amateur Emigrant*. San Francisco was not the end of the journey. He had 150 miles to go to Monterey where Fanny was waiting for her divorce to come through.

He managed to get there more dead than alive, and there was a joyful reunion. Fanny was better, her divorce proceedings, though slow, were going on all right. Stevenson, who felt that he could recover his health most quickly in an outdoor life, bought a horse and rode into the mountains to camp by himself. There he collapsed. He was picked up by two ranchmen, one an old bear hunter and soldier of the American War. They nursed him in the ranch for a fortnight with unfailing kindness until he was able to ride back to Monterey.

There was a happy interval while he lived at the house of a French doctor, dined each night at the restaurant of Jules Simoneau, a gay, philosophic, unsuccessful Frenchman after his own heart, and spent his days with Fanny, but his money was running out, and there seemed no hope of any more. He moved to San Francisco, where he could live more cheaply in a workman's lodging. His friends do not appear to have realised how desperate his condition was. Perhaps in their comfortable, respectable life in London it was difficult to imagine that he was actually going short of food.

They wrote him criticisms of the work he was sending home which, however just, were almost more than he could bear. However, he managed to produce one of his most striking short stories, *The Pavilion on the Links*, which Leslie Stephen accepted at once for the *Cornhill Magazine*. He struggled to the end of *The Amateur Emigrant*, though he admitted that it " bored him hellishly." It is the book of his which comes nearest to boring his readers. He was beginning to realise that travel books were not what he really wanted to write. He wrote an essay on Thoreau and another short story, *A Vendetta in the West*. Anxiety and insufficient food were taking their toll of his fragile body. His landlady's small child, with whom he had made friends, became dangerously ill and he sat up for nights helping to nurse him. The result of all this was a complete collapse, an illness of which he nearly died, and whose effects never wore off. Fanny came to nurse him. Her divorce was now through, and as soon as he could stand they were married, and went to a disused mining camp in the Californian mountains, of which he wrote in *Silverado Squatters*. The doctor had given him only a few months, but he recovered surprisingly in sunshine and happiness.

The news that he had been so near death was too much for the parents who really loved him. They wired him money and forgiveness, and promised to welcome their daughter-in-law. Whatever she might be, she was now his wife and it was their duty to accept her.

Fanny's daughter, Belle, was by now married and had a child, but Lloyd, eleven years old, was a valued part of the new family. Just a year after he set sail from Glasgow, Stevenson, with his wife and stepson, went back home.

CHAPTER IV

THE PROFESSIONAL AUTHOR

THE return to Scotland marked for Stevenson, in life if not in letters, the end of his experimental period. He was married, his difficulties and disagreements with his parents were over, and his relationship with his father from that time onwards was one of affection and peace, partly no doubt because he was established as an adult with a separate family of his own, and partly because Fanny got on extremely well with both her in-laws, and made a conquest especially of Thomas Stevenson. What was she like ? She looks out at us from her portraits, square, dark, determined, formidable, with good dark eyes set wide apart, a most resolute, perhaps an obstinate chin and a firm but not ungenerous mouth. She looks as if she meant to have her own way. To Henley she was somebody who dominated and possessed Stevenson. There is no doubt that she, or the deep-rooted jealousy she roused in Henley, was the rock on which that ardent friendship split. The Colvins were delighted with her, finding her a character " as strong, interesting and romantic as her husband's." To him she was everything that he had foreseen when he stood in the forest of Fontainebleau outside the inn and looked into the lighted room. Instinct was triumphantly vindicated. It was an extremely happy marriage. Stevenson did not often speak or write of his feelings for her, but in a letter written two years before his death, he said, " As I look back, I think my marriage was the best move I ever made in my life." " I love my wife," he wrote, " I do not know how much, nor can, nor shall, unless I lost her." To some of the friends of his bachelor days she seemed to have clipped his wings and to dominate his personality too much. It is a thing which devoted friends are apt to feel about any marriage, but there seems no doubt that Stevenson, luckier in his Fanny than Keats in his, was far happier and more integrated with her than he had ever been before.

His wings were clipped severely by his health. From his first American journey until the last four years in the South Seas he was obliged to live the life of an invalid prostrated by any cold or chill, and liable to sudden hæmorrhages of the lungs. Only once, just before his death, did he admit to Lloyd Osbourne how much he hated the invalid life and how keenly he had felt the " physical degradation," but there was little direct sign of the kind of life he had to live in his writing, indeed he was determined that there should not be. The root of his sometimes almost too exuberant philosophy was his determination not to whine. He felt that whining was a disgrace, and " his feelings," said Henry James, " are always his reasons." That he lived on the edge of death probably had an indirect influence on his writing, for the lines were always clear and the colours vivid. He saw and felt sharply as men feel and see in danger.

Something should be said here about his attitude to his work. He was an artist, who cared passionately for the quality of what he wrote and spent his whole life trying to write better. He was also a moralist who believed it to be his duty to earn his own living, and a living for his wife and stepson. This is no place for the familiar discussion as to whether the two aims are compatible, nor for the fashionable consideration of how much money a writer needs to live on. What is relevant is Stevenson's attitude to the problem, and the way in which it affected his work. In his *Letter to a Young Gentleman who Proposes to Embrace the Career of Art*, an essay which might with advantage be read and even learnt by heart by any aspiring young writer, since it states so clearly the problem of the professional author, Stevenson sets down the articles of his faith.

First, the mark of the writer's calling is his laborious partiality for his Art, " this inextinguishable zest in its technical successes, and (perhaps above all) a certain candour of mind to take his every trifling enterprise with a gravity that would befit the cares of empire, and to think the smallest improvement worth accomplishing at any expense of time and industry. Is it worth doing ? When it shall have occurred to any artist to ask himself that question, it is implicitly answered in the negative."

Secondly, the writer's first reward is the work itself, and not what he gets for it. " The direct return, the wages of the trade, are small, but the indirect, the wages of the life, are incalculably great. No other business offers a man his daily bread upon such joyful terms." " I take the author with whose career I am best acquainted ; and it is true he writes in a rebellious material, and that the act of writing is cramped and trying to both the eyes and the temper ; but remark him in his study, when matter crowds upon him and words are not wanting—in what a continual series of small successes time flies by ; with what a sense of power, as of one moving mountains, he marshals his petty characters ; with what pleasures, both of the eye and ear, he sees his airy structure growing on the page ; how he labours in a craft to which the whole material of his life is tributary, and which opens a door to all his tastes, his loves, his hatreds, his convictions. so that what he writes is only what he longed to utter. He may have enjoyed many things in this big, tragic playground of a world, but what shall he have enjoyed more fully than a morning of successful work ? Suppose it ill paid, the wonder is that it should be paid at all ! Other men pay and pay dearly for pleasures less desirable."

Thirdly, he points out to the young writer that he " works entirely upon honour. The public knows little or nothing of these merits in the quest of which you are condemned to spend the bulk of your endeavours. Merits of design, the merit of first-hand energy, the merit of a certain cheap accomplishment which a man of artistic temper easily acquires ; these they can recognise and these they value. But to these more exquisite refinements of proficiency and finish which the artist so ardently desires and so keenly feels, for which in the vigorous words of Balzac he must toil like a miner buried in a land slip—for which day after day he recasts and revises and rejects, the gross mass of the public must be ever blind. To those lost pains, suppose you attain to the highest pitch of merit, posterity may possibly do justice ; suppose, as is so probable, you fail by a hair's-breadth of the highest, certain it shall never be observed. Under the shadow of this cold thought alone in his studio the artist must preserve from day to day his constancy to his ideals. It is this which makes his life noble."

Then follow two warnings. First against laziness. The artist who says, "It will do," is on the downward path. "By the practice of journalism, a man runs the risk of becoming wedded to cheap finish." But a man's first duty in this world is to pay his way. The young writer must not expect to do this by " making and swallowing artistic formulæ and perhaps falling in love with some particular proficiency of his own." If he proposes to live by his writing and cannot write what people want to read, it is no use exclaiming against the ignorant bourgeois. " To give the public what they do not want and yet expect to be supported, we have here a strange pretension ! " In fact, if the young man feels that by writing what will earn his living, he will falsify his talent, he had better earn his living by some other profession.

There is a word about the prospects of old age. " The devil in these trades of pleasing is to fail to please. The writer has the double misfortune to be ill paid while he can write, and to be incapable of writing when he is old." Then follows the warning which should be to every writer wha tthe oath of Hippocrates is to the doctor. " If you adopt an art to be your trade, weed your mind at the outset of all desire for money. What you may decently expect if you have some talent and much industry, is such an income as a clerk will earn with a tenth and perhaps a twentieth of your nervous output. Nor have you any right to look for more : in the wages of life, not in the wages of your trade, lies your reward. The work is here the wages. . . . If a man be not frugal, he has no business in the arts. If he be not frugal, he will find it hard to continue honest. Some day when the butcher is knocking at the door, he may be tempted, he may be obliged, to turn out and sell a slovenly piece of work."

He concludes with a word about " the delights of popu-larity." " In so far as you mean the countenance of other artists, you would put your finger on one of the most essential and enduring pleasures of the career of art. But in so far as you have an eye to the commendation of the public and the notices of the newspapers, be sure you would be cherishing a dream ! It is true that in certain esoteric journals, the author, for instance, is duly criticised, and that he is often praised a great deal more than he deserves, sometimes for qualities which he prided himself on eschewing, sometimes by ladies and gentlemen who have denied themselves the privilege of reading his work. A man may have done well for years and then fail ; he will hear of his failures. Or he may have done well for years and still do well, but the critics may have tired of praising him, and there may have sprung up some new idol of the instant to whom they now prefer to offer sacrifice. Here is the obverse and reverse of that empty and ugly thing called popularity. Will any man suppose it worth gaining ? "

This was the creed by which Stevenson lived. His double purpose was to write better and to make himself independent of his father. He had gone out to America both to marry Fanny and to stand on his own feet, and, a good deal because he was handicapped by ill-health, he had failed in the latter. He came back to the fight.

CHAPTER V

" TREASURE ISLAND "

THE trend of his work was changing. In the first few weeks after his return, he laboriously put together and polished *The Amateur Emigrant*, which still bored him. His father thought the book not likely to help Louis' reputation, and perhaps did not want the world to read the shifts to which his son had been reduced. He paid to have *The Amateur Emigrant* withdrawn, and it was not published until fourteen years afterwards. The doctors agreed that Stevenson must not risk a northern winter, and in October he went to Davos with Fanny and Lloyd Osbourne, a dog in one basket and a cat in another.

At Davos he found John Addington Symonds, and had the pleasure of another writer's company. It was not an unmixed pleasure. Stevenson was over-awed by Symonds' learning and seems for once in his life to have had something like an inferiority complex. As a rule, he rejoiced as delightedly in the gifts and achievements of his friends as in his own, but he seems to have been a trifle subdued by this contact with an academic mind, the more so that he was not in the mood for his own work. He was exhausted by all his journeys and emotions, and must have been depressed by finding out that his illness had left a chronic weakness of the lungs. He fell into a lethargy, in which, since he was never the man to give up, he managed to produce his *Essay on the Morality of the Profession of Letters* and several other articles. Perhaps the lethargy was not only due to fatigue and depression. An author often has a period of frustration before a fresh outburst of creative energy. Stevenson planned at this time to write a history of the Highlands, and did a lot of reading for it which was afterwards to supply the background of *Kidnapped* and *Catriona*.

When he came back to Scotland in May of the next year, he was still preoccupied with his history of the Highlands, but what he wrote, when they were settled in a cottage in Braemar, was *Thrawn Janet*, one of his best short stories, in fact one of the best supernatural stories ever written. It appeared in the *Cornhill*, to his surprise, for he had thought it too Scots for an English magazine, but Leslie Stephen knew a masterpiece when he saw one. Stevenson also wrote the greater part of *The Merry Men*. This again is one of his best short stories, though he himself thought that it did not come off as a tale, only as a picture of the cruelty and terror of the sea on a wild coast. He was swinging, without noticing it, into fiction. He still visualised himself as a historian, and even went so far as to put in for the Chair of History at Edinburgh University, collecting a bunch of glowing testimonials from his literary friends, who abandoned all scruples about his suitability in the attempt to get Louis anything he wanted.

It was not his literary friends this time who were to give him his lucky break. The weather was appalling. It was impossible to do much out of doors, and Lloyd Osbourne, home for the holidays, was hard up for amusement. With a shilling box of water colours he turned one room in the cottage into an Art Gallery. Stevenson, always ready to play with him, joined in the game, and the two of them spent many hours colouring their drawings.

One rainy morning Lloyd had drawn a map of an island,

Stevenson strolled into the room, looked over his shoulder, and began to elaborate it, writing on the child's drawing the names that were to pass into English Letters, "Skeleton Island," "Spyglass Hill." He put three red crosses in one corner of the island, and wrote across the top of the map the words "Treasure Island." He did not answer when Lloyd spoke to him. He muttered something about pirates, and buried treasure and a man marooned on the island. Lloyd clamoured for a story, and was surprised and chagrined when his stepfather pocketed his map and walked away without speaking.

Stevenson has told us in his own words what happened. "No child but must remember laying his head in the grass, staring into the infinitesimal forest and seeing it grow populous with fairy armies. Somewhat in this way, as I pored upon the map of Treasure Island, the future characters of the book began to appear there visibly among imaginary woods, their brown faces and bright weapons peeping out upon me from unexpected quarters as they passed to and fro fighting and hunting treasure on those few square inches of a flat projection. The next thing I knew I had some paper before me and was writing out a list of characters."

He began it next morning and wrote a chapter a day until he was half-way through. It was his first spontaneous book, coming crisp as a biscuit from the oven of his mind where the fires burned always steadily but sometimes too low. In the evenings he read aloud what he had written to Lloyd Osbourne and to his father who was staying with them. Thomas Stevenson was as much delighted as the boy. It was his kind of picturesque. When the time came for Billy Bones' sea chest to be ransacked, he spent the better part of a day preparing on the back of an old envelope an inventory of the contents which Louis used in the book. Probably Louis had few happier hours than those evenings when he read aloud work which was really admired by his father, the man whom, as he admitted, he loved next to his wife, more than any of his friends.

There is no need here to summarise *Treasure Island*, so well known to millions as a book, as a play, as a film. It is the perfect example of its kind. Readers in almost every language have seen the brown old seaman with the sabre-cut plodding to the inn door, his sea chest following him on a hand barrow ; have trembled with Jim Hawkins at the tapping of Blind Pew's stick ; have crouched in the apple barrel with Jim and heard the words that came as a revealing shock. " ' No, not I,' said Silver, ' Flint was cap'n. I was quartermaster.' " Millions of readers have heard the sudden scream of the loyal seamen rise above the booming surf of the Island ; the shriek of Silver's parrot ; and the thin far voice of Ben Gunn echoing Flint's death-cry, "Darby M'Graw ! Darby M'Graw ! Fetch aft the rum, Darby ! " Everything in *Treasure Island* is appropriate, everything strikes to the nerves of the reader as being right. So and no other island would have looked, so and no other the Squire, the Doctor, the Captain and Long John Silver would have behaved, and not only the story but the vigour, economy and liveliness of the writing have attracted many a grown-up reader. Within its own limitations *Treasure Island* is art, it is magic. We feel that the thing could not have been different, it could not have been done better. Perhaps it is not straining a boy's book too far to remark that this, Stevenson's first novel, was in the pattern that was to develop in his later work. *Treasure Island*, too, is a morality. The good men put down the bad men, the bad men are in rebellion like the fallen angels, and declare themselves, as Mr. Hyde did later, by the sickening sin of cruelty. Long John Silver is the most striking character in the book, and the Captain is a dry figure of a martinet, but our hearts are never with Long John again after his crutch has flown across the green dell pinning an innocent man to the ground.

Treasure Island, when only half-finished (accepted as a serial by *Young Folks*), began to appear. It was less popular with the juvenile subscribers than several serials that had preceded it. It is doubtful whether children do like well-written books better than badly written books any more than they would like old brandy better than a jelly. Stevenson's friends, Gosse and Henley, read *Treasure Island* as it came out, and *Young Folks* must have added some distinguished names to the list of subscribers. Stevenson told Henley that his " maimed masterfulness had given him the germ from which Long John Silver grew." He stuck in the middle of the book, to his alarm. " My mouth was empty, there was not one word more of *Treasure Island* in my bosom." He was the more appalled because the early chapters were already appearing and it was time to leave Scotland for winter quarters. " I was indeed very close on despair, but I shut my mouth hard and during the journey had the resolution to think of other things. Arrived at my destination, down I sat one morning at the unfinished tale, and behold, it flowed from me like small talk ; and in a second tide of delighted industry, and at a rate of a chapter a day, I finished *Treasure Island*."

CHAPTER VI

THE ART OF FICTION

THE Stevensons went back to Davos for the winter. The place bored Louis, who hated being anywhere cold, however good for his lungs. High altitudes did not agree with Fanny: she became really ill and twice had to leave him for a time to the distinguished but slightly damping company of John Addington Symonds, who looked askance at *Treasure Island*—or Stevenson thought he did—and wanted him to write on the characters of Theophrastus. Lloyd Osbourne and his toy printing press and regiments of tin soldiers were more congenial company. They conducted elaborate military operations, and Stevenson wrote verses, and drew and cut the woodcuts which Lloyd published on his Davos press and sold for a penny, blissfully unaware that in May 1923 they were to fetch about £50 each at Sotheby's. " I would send you one," Louis wrote to Edmund Gosse, " but I declare I am ruined ! I get a penny a cut and a half-penny a set of verses from the flint-hearted publisher and only one specimen copy as I'm a sinner ! "

In spite of his dislike for Davos, his health improved and he had a much better winter's work. After finishing *Treasure Island* in a fortnight, he wrote up *Silverado Squatters* from his notebook. This account of his strange honeymoon in a mining camp in California is the least personal but one of the most charming of his travel books. His faculty for picking up odd acquaintances wherever he went and for striking sparks of character out of them was never more pleasantly displayed. He wrote, as always, superbly of weather and

open country, and his happiness with Fanny and in the return
from illness and town life to a measure of health and activity
out of doors sings in the pages, though he says little of either.
On that holiday everything pleased him. "I liked to draw
water. It was pleasant to dip the grey metal pail into the
clean, colourless, cool water ; pleasant to carry it back with
the water lipping at the edge and a broken sunbeam quivering
in the midst."

In this winter at Davos he also wrote *Talk and Talkers*,
and *A Gossip on Romance*, in which he defined what he
was aiming at in writing fiction. He believed that the first
purpose of fiction was to delight the reader, and that the most
intense delight comes when the reader pushes the hero aside
and identifies himself with him, plunging into the tale in his
own person.

"Fiction is to the grown man what play is to the child,
it is there he changes the atmosphere and tenor of his life,
and when the game so chimes with his fancy that he can
join in it with all his heart, when it pleases him with every
turn, when he lives to recall it and dwells on its recollection
with entire delight, fiction is called Romance." The heart of
this romance, Stevenson believes, is action. "The right kind
of thing should fall out in the right kind of place ; the right
kind of thing should follow ; and all the circumstances in a
tale answer one another like notes in music. The threads of
a story come from time to time together, and make a picture
in the web, the characters fall into some attitude to each other
and to nature which stamps the story home like an illustration.
Crusoe recoiling before the footprint, Achilles shouting over
against the Trojans, Ulysses bending the great bow, Christian
running with his fingers in his ears. These are the cul-
minating moments in the legend, and each has been printed

on the mind's eye for ever. Other things we may forget ; we may forget the words, although they are beautiful ; we may forget the author's comment, although perhaps it was ingenious and true ; but these epoch-making scenes, which put the last mark of truth upon a story and fill up at overflow our capacity for sympathetic pleasure, we so adopt into the very bosom of our mind that neither time nor tide can efface or weaken the impression. This, then, is the highest, the plastic part of literature ; to embody character, thought or emotion in some act or attitude that shall be remarkably striking to the mind's eye." "In character studies," he goes on to say, " the pleasure that we take is critical . . . it is in the action and incident that we lose ourselves in the character."

He is, in fact, frankly defending literature of escape. He never had any sympathy with the literary Puritanism that would make something between a tract and a documentary of a novel. He saw clearly that realism is only part of reality. To him it did not matter whether a book was literature of escape or not, only whether it was literature. He makes it clear, however, that the delight which a work of art can give is not confined to " all that is grouped under the name of comedy."

" It is not only pleasurable things that we imagine in our day-dreams ; there are lights in which we are willing to contemplate even the idea of our death ; ways in which it seems as if it would amuse us to be cheated, wounded or calumniated." Tragedy can be as satisfying as comedy, sometimes more so since what the human being craves most is not happiness but experience.

No man respected art or the practice of his particular art more than Stevenson, but he was never portentous about it.

Not only does he think that realism is not the first aim of fiction, he sees that it is not attainable. In "A Humble Remonstrance" addressed to Henry James, "No art," he says, "can compete with life. To compete with life, whose sun we cannot look upon, whose passions and diseases waste and slay us—to compete with the flavour of wine, the beauty of the dawn, the scorching of fire, the bitterness of death and separation—here is, indeed, a projected escalade of Heaven! No Art is true in this sense nor can compete with life, not even history, built indeed of indisputable facts, but these facts robbed of their vivacity and sting, so that even when we read of the sack of a city and the fall of an empire, we are surprised, and justly commend the author's talent, if our pulse be quickened. And mark, for a last differentiation this quickening of the pulse is, in almost every case, purely agreeable. That these phantom reproductions of experience, even at their most acute, convey decided pleasure ; while experience itself in the cockpit of life can torture and slay."

In the spring Chatto and Windus published a book of Stevenson's essays under the title *Familiar Studies of Men and Books*. They also published the *New Arabian Nights* in book form. Stevenson came back to Scotland for the summer, the last time that he was to return and spend a summer in his native climate.

There are some who think the *New Arabian Nights* the best of Stevenson's work. The idea of the Suicide Club first arose in conversation between Louis and his cousin Robert Alan (Bob) Stevenson, the artist, and Bob was, according to Fanny, the model of the "Young Man with the Cream Tarts" ; while Prince Florizel was Stevenson's conception of Edward VII, then Prince of Wales. "Yes," he wrote to Bob Stevenson, "I remember the *enfantement* of the *Arabian*

Nights. The first idea of all was the hansom cabs. The same afternoon the Prince de Galles and the Suicide Club were invented ; and several more now forgotten." The stories tell the fantastic adventures of Prince Florizel of Bohemia, who, in the romantic tradition, wanders incognito with a companion in London and Paris and stumbles upon the Suicide Club, an association of men determined to die who draw lots for death. The pursuit and punishment of the President of the Club, the man who exploits a suicidal mood until it becomes an inescapable purpose, expands into a story of fantastic adventures, with the strange logic and the vivid colouring of dreams. The Rajah's diamond provides the connecting thread for the second series of stories, until Prince Florizel, who never quite forgets that his creator is a moralist, throws it into the waters of the Seine.

Stevenson was advised not to publish these stories in book form as they were too fantastic and likely to injure his reputation. Fanny remarks in a preface to a later edition of the volume, " There was not a single story, poem, article, or novel written by my husband that was not similarly condemned by some of his friends and literary advisers."

During this winter in Davos he began to write the verses which he then called "Penny Whistles," but which he afterwards published as the *Child's Garden of Verses*. They were a diversion when he was not equal to any other work, for although his lungs were better at Davos, his spirits were very low. He hated his invalid life in this invalid place. He was miserable when Fanny was obliged to leave him, and his distress at making so little money and at being still partly dependent on his father weighed heavily on his mind.

" I do not know what is to become of us," he wrote to Charles Baxter. " My wife is worse and worse, now sent away with Lloyd, I not being allowed to go down. I don't care for solitude as I used to ; results, I suppose, of marriage. Oh for Edinburgh ! But here, a sheer hulk lies poor Tom Bowling and aspires, yes, C.B., with tears, after the past ! See what comes of being left alone." He was near despair, but he did not give up the struggle. By April he wrote that since December he had written 40,000 words of essays and stories, " and I am none the worse. I am better. I begin to hope that I may, if not outlive this wolverine on my shoulders, at least carry him bravely." He came back to Scotland for another summer in the Highlands, but the weather was so bad that he was hardly able to go out of doors. He was sick of repulses and invalidism, but he wrote the first draft of his short story, *The Treasure of Franchard*, in a belated month of fine weather which cheated him into believing that he might be able to spend summers in Scotland after all. A hæmorrhage in early September put this out of the question for ever, and since neither he nor Fanny could face the thought of Davos again, they went to the South of France to look for a home.

CHAPTER VII

HYÈRES

THE search for a house in the South of France was at first unlucky. Fanny was still not strong enough to knock about, and Stevenson, who was hardly more fit for it, went with his cousin Bob to find a house in Montpellier. He was again taken ill there with lung trouble. He struggled to Marseilles, where Fanny joined him, and they found a house about five miles out at St. Marcel. The place did not suit him and an epidemic of fever drove them away. They went to Hyères, and by March had got into a house, Chalet la Solitude. It stood on the slope of the hill on which the castle stands. It was very small, " with a garden like a fairy story and a view like a classical landscape."

Here they stayed for nearly a year, which later Stevenson said had been the happiest year in his life. He wrote to Gosse, " I dwell already the next door to heaven. If you could see my roses, and my big marigolds, and my olives, and my view over a plain, and my view of certain mountains as graceful as Apollo, as severe as Zeus, you would not think the phrase exaggerated."

To his mother he wrote about Fanny with unusual freedom, " I love her better than ever and admire her more, and I cannot think what I have done to deserve so good a gift. This sudden remark came out of my pen, it is not like me ; but in case you did not know, I may as well tell you that my marriage has been the most successful in the world."

He had also the beginnings of a wider recognition for his work to make him happy. In May, Cassells offered to publish

Treasure Island in book form, and astonished him by proposing to pay an advance of a hundred pounds. " A hundred pounds all alive O ! A hundred jingling, tingling, golden, minted quid ! Is not this wonderful ? " " Really," he said in a letter to Henley, " a hundred pounds is a sight more than *Treasure Island* is worth." The *Century Magazine* in New York also accepted *Silverado Squatters*, his first real contract with any American publisher. He was beginning work on *Prince Otto*, a scheme for a novel of the kind later called Ruritanian, with which he had been playing for a year or two.

At first *Prince Otto* went well. " My head is singing with *Otto*," he wrote to Henley. It was always one of his favourite books and he put an immense amount of effort into it. He rewrote one chapter seven times before he laid it aside to undertake a commission which Fanny opposed vigorously, and about which for once he himself was cynical. The editor of *Young Folks* asked him to write another serial story for children. Some years before he had made a study of the fifteenth century and read among other things the Paston Letters. He used this material now for *The Black Arrow*, a historical tale of the Wars of the Roses, which included a portrait of Richard Crookback whose age Stevenson, for once as immoral as Scott, advanced by several years for the convenience of his story. He spoke of *The Black Arrow* as " tushery." It was not the spontaneous creation that *Treasure Island* had been. It was an honest bit of work with which, as always, he did his best, but it was perhaps the only work he ever undertook against his better judgment. The money offered was not much, but it was immediate payment by instalments, and so served for those payments to butcher and baker which Stevenson always saw as his first duty. He dedicated it to the uncompromising Fanny, critic on the hearth, because " it is the only book of mine which you have never read, and never will read." The child subscribers to *Young Folks* liked *The Black Arrow* better than *Treasure Island*.

Treasure Island was published as a book in November 1884, and though the sales were not at first large—about 5000 in the first year—it made a reputation for Stevenson outside the small *Cornhill* circle who had always admired his work. The Editor of the *Saturday Review* wrote that *Treasure Island* was the best book that had appeared since *Robinson Crusoe*. " I don't know," said Andrew Lang, " that since *Tom Sawyer* and the *Odyssey,* I ever liked any romance so well." The great Mr. Gladstone picked up the book in a friend's house and scoured London the next day for a copy. Stephen Gwynn, author of *R.L.S.* in the "English Men of Letters" Series, recalls how as an undergraduate at Brasenose he took the book to read in his second-floor bedroom, and was obliged in the small hours to get up and hunt for a fresh candle, when he found himself " quivering with excitement from head to foot." Stevenson was, of course, pleased and encouraged, but remarked in a letter to his parents, " This gives one strange thoughts of how bad the common run of books must be ! " He was in a sober mood, for a life-long friend, Walter Ferrier, had just died of consumption, and this was not only a sorrow, but an underlining of the menace with which Stevenson himself lived.

Persistent as always, he nearly finished *Prince Otto* before his friends, Henley and Charles Baxter, came out to spend a holiday with him in the New Year. The house was too small to hold them comfortably, and with Louis and Fanny they went on a visit to Nice. Stevenson caught cold and immediately went down with congestion of the lungs. The doctor told his wife that there was no hope, but he recovered, though very slowly, and with the complications of ophthalmia and sciatica to add to the ever-present risk of hæmorrhage. He was obliged to lie in the dark without speaking or moving his right arm. In this condition he was undaunted. Fanny made up to amuse him the tales which they afterwards published under their two names as *The Dynamiters*, and he himself wrote more of the *Child's Garden of Verses*, labouriously printing the verses on a board in large letters with his left hand. He also wrote his best-known poem, " Requiem," which is carved on his grave in Samoa.

> Under the wide and starry sky
> Dig the grave and let me lie,
> Glad did I live and gladly die
> And I laid me down with a will.
>
> This be the verse you grave for me,
> Here he lies where he longed to be,
> Home is the sailor, home from sea,
> And the hunter home from the hill.

As soon as he was able to travel he and Fanny came back to England and took rooms at Bournemouth, where Lloyd Osbourne was at school.

CHAPTER VIII

"PRINCE OTTO"

STEVENSON lived in Bournemouth for nearly three years, first in temporary quarters, then in a house presented to him by his father, which he christened " Skerryvore," the name of the most famous lighthouse built by his family, on the western coast of Scotland. Skerryvore was a neat suburban villa in a suburban district, and according to Lloyd Osbourne, Stevenson never really liked it, but there were fir trees near the house which reminded him of the Highlands, and the view from the front of the curves of the bay bore a faint resemblance to his beloved Mediterranean coast. It was a pleasure to Fanny to settle down and be a householder ; it was even a pleasure for a time to the restless Stevenson, though with him anyone could have foretold that it was not likely to last.

The three years were chequered. He wrote at Bournemouth *Dr. Jekyll and Mr. Hyde*, the first book to bring him a wide public. He wrote *Kidnapped*, one of his best novels, considered his best so far by Henry James, with whom he engaged at this time in a friendly public duel on the art of fiction. He enjoyed being near his friends in London, who were able to run down and see him whenever he was fit for it. On the debit side, his health was wretched. He had frequent hæmorrhages and lived under the constant threat of them. He was only able to go away occasionally to people who were willing to take this risk, as the Colvins were in their house by the British Museum, which he called the " Monument." His father, whom he so deeply loved, was failing, and in a constant depression of spirits. His friendship with Henley, one of the best things in his life, was running less smoothly, the stress of collaboration in plays which neither of them could write bringing to the surface in Henley that double feeling which so often exists in a vivid relationship. He had never forgiven Stevenson for marrying Fanny, and Fanny did not like him.

The two friends had begun to write for the theatre before Stevenson came to live in England. *Deacon Brodie*, a play about an Edinburgh character who was a respectable cabinet-maker by day and a burglar by night, was put on in July 1884, but had no success, critical or box office. Stevenson, restless in writing as in life, was always willing to try anything new, but he had less faith in their dramatic abilities than Henley, and his candid admission of their failures probably annoyed his fellow playwright more than he realised.

During the first months in Bournemouth Stevenson felt that, although *Deacon Brodie* was a failure, they might yet produce something better. They wrote two more plays, *Admiral Guinea* and *Beau Austin*, and planned several others which they never wrote. Stevenson then went back to his own work and finished *Prince Otto*. He is a difficult author to follow chronologically. He began books, broke off, started others that he never finished and then went back to the old work, wrote and rewrote, set it aside and suddenly took it up again and completed it. His vicissitudes in health and constant changes of scene, prompted by the restlessness of the consumptive, make anyone who attempts a straight-forward chronicle feel that he is clinging to the tail of a moving star.

Prince Otto was published in 1885 after running as a serial in *Longman's Magazine*. It was much dearer to its author than

4

it has been to most of his admirers. It is a light, tinkling charade, written brilliantly and sometimes exquisitely, but never for one moment carrying conviction. Artificial as the shepherdesses of the Trianon, Otto, his princess and their surrounding court play their parts like skilfully handled puppets and never take on the semblance of flesh and blood. At first Stevenson meant to use Otto to portray the character of his favourite cousin, Bob Stevenson. Later he decided that Otto was like himself. Except in having eyes of a darker colour than his hair, a certain charm, and a habit of picking up acquaintances on a journey, the likeness is hard to find. Otto was a spineless, wastrel princeling who had no conception of his duty to his subjects and spent his time in hunting, while his throne slipped through his fingers and his young wife became the tool and was thought to have become the mistress of a scheming politician. When he noticed the situation, Otto showed a flash of spirit, took control for half an hour, and then threw up the sponge because a friend criticised him, and absconded from his kingdom. The surge of revolution sent his wife wandering to the forest, where he found her, and then they lived happy ever afterwards as hangers-on at various European courts. " The moral," Stevenson wrote, " lies precisely in the freeing of two spirits from court intrigues."

Strange that Stevenson, so conscious of responsibility, so strenuous of purpose, and for all his fragility, so much a man, should have fancied that he had drawn his own likeness in this featherweight who could put up no sort of fight for his work or his wife's honour ! Stevenson was generally ready to accept criticism of his books, often the first to apply it, but when a bad review of Otto appeared in the Saturday Review, he said in a letter to Henley that the reviewer was dull, and contested his points. Henley reviewed the book with a gush of over-praise, as Stevenson saw. Henley was probably swinging between two extremes of feeling for his friend.

The first year in Bournemouth was prolific. After finishing *Prince Otto*, Stevenson also finished *A Child's Garden of Verses*, and, with Fanny, *More New Arabian Nights*. In this year he began *Kidnapped*, designed at first as a story for boys. He planned a novel about highwaymen, never to be written, called *The Great North Road*. He also planned to write the life of Wellington for a series edited by Andrew Lang. He had all his life a great admiration for soldiers, and was keenly interested in military history, but although he received the suggestion of this book with rapture, he never wrote it. In the summer his old friend and professor, Fleeming Jenkin, died, and Stevenson began to write a Memoir of him to be published with his collected works. This year he also wrote as a Christmas story, *Olalla*, the tale of an English volunteer in the Carlist War who went to recuperate from his wounds in a remote house among the Spanish mountains where he found the remnant of an old family, crazy mother, half-witted son, and beautiful daughter with whom he fell in love at first sight but who sent him away from her so that he should not share her inheritance of madness. This story was based on a dream which broke off when the soldier and the girl met and instantly fell in love. It loses power after their meeting, and Stevenson was not able to finish it with the same colour and conviction that had pervaded the dream material. He himself said that *Olalla* was " not real," but he could not tell why. *Markheim*, which he also wrote in this year, was real, he said, but *Olalla* was not, and it was hard to tell what made reality. *Markheim* was inspired by an article on the subconscious which Stevenson had read in a

French scientific journal. Markheim calls at a fence's shop on Christmas Day under pretence of buying a Christmas present for a lady with whom he hopes to make a rich marriage. He stabs the dealer and runs upstairs to steal his money before the servant comes home. While he is rummaging for it, another character, his own unconscious, appears in his likeness, and taunts him with the hopelessness of his position and the inevitable decline of his life into further wickedness. He must, for instance, begin to assure his safety by murdering the servant, who is to be heard at the door. To prevent himself from committing more crimes, Markheim decides that he will give up his life—" my love of good is damned to barrenness, but I still have my hatred of evil ! " The features of the supernatural visitor begin to " undergo a wonderful and lovely change ; they lightened and softened with a tender triumph." Markheim meets the servant at the door. " You had better go for the police ; I have killed your master."

Was it before he wrote this that he read *Crime and Punishment*, of which he wrote so enthusiastically to John Addington Symonds in the spring of next year ? Both the murder and the expiation suggest an unconscious association. Stevenson was at this time taking a good deal of laudanum, which was prescribed by his doctor in the hope of preventing hæmorrhages. He was also, for the first time in his life, finding it difficult to sleep. His mind was endlessly preoccupied with " the only thing I feel dreadful about, that damned old business of the war in the members." Some conflict was working its way upwards, and the laudanum, if it did not prevent the hæmorrhages, was to give him a stranger dream than *Olalla*, a stronger story than *Markheim*.

CHAPTER IX

"DR. JEKYLL AND MR. HYDE"

FANNY was startled awake in the night by cries of horror. It was Louis who was crying out in his sleep. She roused him, and he protested, "Why did you wake me? I was dreaming a fine bogey tale!" Next morning he gave orders that he was not to be interrupted, even if the house caught fire. For three days he wrote without stopping, sitting up in bed and covering page after page. At the end of three days he came downstairs and read aloud to Fanny and Lloyd the first draft of *Dr. Jekyll and Mr. Hyde.*

Lloyd listened to it, he says, spellbound, and waited for his mother's outburst of enthusiasm at the end of the reading. It did not come. Her praise was constrained, her words seemed to come with difficulty. Then all at once, she broke into criticism. Louis had missed the point. He had not brought out the allegory. He had made it a story, but it should have been a masterpiece. Stevenson was furious. He trembled with rage, argued violently, then rushed out of the room. Fanny sat by the fire, pale and miserable, staring into the flames. After a time they heard Stevenson coming downstairs again. Lloyd, who thought his mother wrong and sympathised with his stepfather, dreaded a fresh quarrel. But Stevenson said, "You're right, I've missed the allegory, which is, after all, the whole point of it." He threw the manuscript into the flames. They both cried out, and tried to save it, thinking that he had done it in pique, but he denied it. "In trying to save some of it, I should have got

53

hopelessly off the track. The only way was to put temptation beyond my reach." Three more days while he sat up in bed, writing, writing, writing, sheet after sheet of paper falling on the counterpane. He hardly spoke at meals. He disappeared in the evenings. His household went about on tiptoe, holding their breath. In three days the second draft was finished. The copying by hand, a considerable labour in those years before typewriting, took two days more. On the sixth the book went off to Longmans. Stevenson had written sixty-four thousand words in six days, and whatever the first draft may have been like, Fanny's interference was probably justified, for *Dr. Jekyll and Mr. Hyde* was a small masterpiece.

Faust, when he sold his soul to the devil, found that he had to pay the devil's price. Henry Jekyll discovered a drug which enabled him to shed his respectable daytime personality, and even his body. He could go about doing evil in the hours of darkness in the unrecognisable shape of Edward Hyde. The story is built up at first from the outside as each fresh piece of astonishing evidence came to the knowledge of Utterson, the decent, kindly lawyer who was Jekyll's oldest friend. The ordinariness and sobriety of his life and character intensify the horror, which is present from the first scene in a London back street on a Sunday evening where Utterson and Enfield see Hyde knock down a child and trample wantonly on the fallen body. Both the lawyer and the cheerful young man-about-town are struck cold, feeling the presence of more than natural evil, and the doctor who is called to the child, " a dry apothecary with a strong Edinburgh accent, and about as emotional as a bagpipe," turns white every time he looks at Hyde. The scenery is mostly laid in solid, dignified houses, elderly

gentlemen dine together, and take their glass of wine by the
fire, respectful servants answer the door. Only once again
is Hyde seen to commit an act of violent sadism, but evil
is there all the time, a living presence as the mystified and
incredulous Utterson comes more and more to the heart of
the mystery, and discovers that the power invoked by
Henry Jekyll has overpowered him. Not only does the
second drug which Hyde drinks when he wants to become
Jekyll again lose its effect. The brute personality is winning.
The change into Hyde comes upon Jekyll no longer at his
command, but of its own volition. Jekyll has called Hyde
into being, and Jekyll in the end is swamped by Hyde.
When a man sells his soul to the devil, he cannot claim it
back again, and as with Markheim, death is the only cure
for a life of endless wickedness.

It would be easy in the light of modern psychology to
suggest an interpretation of this story which was not known
to Stevenson. Stevenson's ego feared his id. He believed
in the power of evil in his own unconscious nature, and was
afraid that if he allowed it to come up, it would swamp his
whole personality. Any psychologist knows such fears in
his patients, planted there by the conflicts of their early
childhood, and knows that these fears are at least partly
groundless, for the final secret of repression is that the forces
repressed are forces for good as much as for evil. But the
patient does not know it, and Stevenson did not know it.
Here in *Jekyll and Hyde* is the core of his innermost life. " If
I were to unloose the things that I keep battened down, I
should do evil and I would rather die."

Speculation about the effects of neurosis on a writer's
work are interesting and valuable in so far as they deepen
our understanding of the work, but they are secondary to

the quality of the work itself. What matters first about a writer is what he writes. In intensity, in power, in execution, *Dr. Jekyll and Mr. Hyde* is a small masterpiece and one of Stevenson's best books. Springing spontaneously from the deepest level of his being, it does not, as so many of his works do, sag before the climax. Every chapter carries conviction. It was published by Longmans in January 1886, at a shilling, a very unusual venture for those days, but they felt it to be a book which should be within everybody's reach. At once it swept England, and was vigorously pirated in America, where there was still no protection for the English author's copyright. *Dr. Jekyll and Mr. Hyde* became the subject of leading articles and long reviews : it was used as a text in pulpits. Critics received it with startled praise. " I do not know," wrote John Addington Symonds, " whether anyone has the right so to scrutinise the abysmal depth of personality, but the art is burning and intense. How had you the *ilia dura ferro et aere triplici duriora* to write *Dr. Jekyll* ? " Stevenson was now a well-known writer with the wide reputation which made it possible for him to achieve his ambition to keep his own family without help from his father. This success came to him thirteen years after the appearance of his first published work.

CHAPTER X

" KIDNAPPED "

IN January 1886, the same month in which *Dr. Jekyll and Mr. Hyde* was published, Stevenson wrote to his father, " I have no earthly news, living entirely in my story and only coming out of it to play patience." The story was *Kidnapped*, which he had begun and laid aside some months before. He took it up again with renewed interest. " I find it a most picturesque period and wonder Scott let it escape." He adds, " I think David is on his feet and to my mind a far better and sounder story than *Treasure Island*." It was the only one of his books, he tells us, in which the characters took the bit between their teeth : " all at once they became detached from the flat paper . . . from that time my task was stenographic—it was they who spoke, they who wrote the remainder of the story."

The scene is laid in the Highlands of Scotland in the years after the '45 rising. The germ of the novel is the trial of James Stewart for the murder of Colin Campbell, King George's Factor in Appin. Stevenson, always interested in this period of Scottish history, came upon the case by chance in a book of trials which his wife was reading, and there found the character of Alan Breck Stewart, who came over from France, in his blue coat with the silver buttons and feathered hat, to convey the second rent which the Highland clansmen, impoverished though they were, paid voluntarily to support their chieftain in exile. In the end the trial was left over to the sequel, *Catriona*, but the murder of Colin Campbell, the Red Fox, is the key scene of *Kidnapped*.

The novel opens with the young David Balfour setting

out from his village with the Bible, the shilling-piece and the recipe for Lily of the Valley Water as his sole possessions, except for a letter from his dead father to the unknown house of Shaws. David Balfour is a block of integrity. One of the most self-respecting heroes of fiction, he is always nicely balanced between what is due to himself and what is due to other people. He is not aggressive, but he does not allow himself to be put upon. It is a great shock to the boy to find that the rich relation from whom he had hoped for help and advancement dwindles down to the miserly and near crazy Uncle Ebenezer, who lives alone in his empty house and offers to an unwelcome nephew a sup of his own porridge and a drink from his own mug of ale, but when Uncle Ebenezer threatens to show him the door if he attempts to communicate with the friends he has left in the village, David replies at once, " Uncle Ebenezer, I've no manner of reason to suppose you mean anything but well by me. For all that, I would have you to know that I have a pride of my own. It was by no will of mine that I came seeking you, and if you show me the door again, I'll take you at your word." Here in a paragraph is David Balfour, willing to be reasonable, unwilling to be bullied, with sixteen years of moral Scots upbringing and a good home behind him.

It has been said that he was the most like Stevenson of all his characters. A novelist can only make characters out of the stuff in his own mind. Even when he believes that he draws them from observation of real characters, that very observation is coloured by his own vision and transmuted as he writes. Some of the characters are more recognisably like him than others, that is all that can be said. There was a lot of Stevenson left out of David Balfour, and some of it was in Alan Breck Stewart.

David, after a narrow escape from being murdered by his uncle, is kidnapped aboard the brig *Covenant*. The story quickens on that night of fog when the brig runs down a boat, drowning all but one of her crew, who leaps up and catches the bowsprit of the *Covenant*. David has his first view of an ally, to be his travelling companion for many a day and his lifelong friend. If David is solid worth and of a Roman virtue, Alan Breck Stewart is the very essence of the picturesque, "smallish in stature, but well set and as nimble as a goat; his face of a good open expression, but sunburnt very dark, and heavily freckled and pitted with the smallpox; his eyes unusually light, and had a kind of dancing madness in them that was both engaging and alarming; and when he took off his greatcoat, he laid a pair of fine silver-mounted pistols on the table, and I saw that he was belted with a great sword. His manners, besides, were elegant and he pledged the captain handsomely. Altogether I thought him at first sight a man that I would rather have for my friend than my enemy."

There follows the plot against Alan and David, then the battle of the Roundhouse in which each of the two does valiantly and according to his nature. Alan, the tried soldier, defends himself with professional skill and gusto, and being a poet, makes a song about the battle while his sword is still wet. David, who will always be a civilian and a man of law, fights with a reluctant courage and kneels down after the victory, horrified at the sight of the two men he has killed.

The ship is wrecked on the rocks near Mull. David scrambles ashore alone and so begins the journey through the Western Highlands after Alan, who has gone before him.

David's wanderings bring him to Alan again at a critical

moment. The Factor's Cavalcade turns the corner of the road, the big red-bearded man rides towards him, the servant behind him with the net of lemons for making punch at his saddle bow. David starts up out of the heather and asks the way to the House of James of the Glens. While they are questioning him, a shot rings out and the Red Fox falls dead in the road. David sees a figure hastening up the hillside and starts in pursuit. He has seen murder done and his decent soul is outraged. The lawyer cries out, " Ten pounds if you take the lad." He stands still, horrified at a danger which he suddenly perceives, but there is a whisper in his ear, " Jouk in here among the trees." There is Alan with a fishing-rod in his hand. They run through the heather, taking care, as David sees, to show themselves to the soldiers. Afterwards, when he comments on this, he gets a taste of Alan's morality, the morality of a guerilla loyalty so alien to his own law-abiding soul. " You and me," Alan explains, " were innocent of the transaction." " The better reason to get clear," David exclaims. But Alan disagrees, " Why, David, the innocent have aye a chance to get assoiled in court. Them that have nae dipped their hands in any little difficulty should be very mindful of the case of them that have. That is good Christianity." David abandons the argument in that mixture of admiration and exasperation which is to be intensified by the wanderings and fatigues and dangers of their journey to Edinburgh, until it works up into a quarrel after Alan has gambled away what money they have in Cluny's cave. But the friendship is strong enough to survive a quarrel and Alan cements their better understanding. " Just precisely what I thought I liked about ye was that you never quarrelled —and now I like ye better ! " This is the scene that Henry James called a " real stroke of genius with the logic and rhythm of life." The relationship between the two men, their contrasting characters and civilisations are beautifully done and make this far more than the children's book it was meant to be.

The book ends as they come to Edinburgh, and David outfaces his uncle and secures his inheritance. Alan goes into hiding in the woods near Corstorphine, and David, now a man of property, advances upon the city to work out his double purpose, to get Alan safely out of the country and to give the evidence about the murder which he believes may save the life of James Stewart.

In a letter to Watts-Dunton, Stevenson gave his own opinion of the work. " I began it partly as a lark and partly as a pot-boiler ; and suddenly it moved. David and Alan stepped out from the canvas, and I found I was in another world. But there was the cursed beginning and a cursed end must be appended ; and our old friend Byles the butcher was plainly audible tapping at the back door—so it had to go into the world, one part (as it does seem to me) alive, one part galvanised ; no work, only an essay. For a man of tentative method and weak health and a scarcity of private means, and not too much of that frugality which is the artist's proper virtue, the days of sinecures and patrons look very golden ; the days of professional literature very hard— yet I do not so far deceive myself as to think I should change my character by changing my epoch, the sum of virtue in our books is in a relation of equality to the sum of virtue in ourselves ; and my *Kidnapped* was doomed, while still in the womb and while I was yet in the cradle, to be the thing it is." *Kidnapped* was published in 1886, just six months after the publication of *Dr. Jekyll and Mr. Hyde.*

CHAPTER XI

DEATH OF THOMAS STEVENSON

STEVENSON'S great compensation in the years at Bournemouth was that he was able to see more of his literary friends and to make new ones. Colvin, Gosse and Henley were within easy reach. Stevenson, with Fanny, made a visit to Hardy in the West Country. Staying with Colvin at his quarters in the British Museum, Stevenson met Robert Browning and Burne-Jones. Henry James came down to Skerryvore and the two men corresponded about the art of fiction, in private letters as well as in their public exchange in print. Henry James' sketch of R.L.S. in *Partial Portraits*, written with much insight and affection, is one of the best estimates of his quality as a writer, though it was written midway in his career, after *Kidnapped* had appeared, so that it did not include the later novels. Sargent came too, to paint Stevenson—" a portrait of me walking about in my own living-room, in my own velveteen jacket, and twisting, as I go, my own moustache . . . it is, I think, excellent, but too eccentric to be exhibited . . . all touched in lovely with that witty touch of Sargent's, but of course it looks damn queer as a whole." The portrait suggests an animal pacing a cage, and it was the life of a caged animal which Stevenson was leading in those years, shut up in Skerryvore " like a weevil in a biscuit." Nor could any portrait look much queerer than he himself often looked, sitting up writing in a bed scattered with papers, his head thrust through a hole in an old blanket, his hair nearly long enough to touch it, his bright brown eyes shining in his

wasted face. These years, so rich in production, were wretched
in health, and Stevenson was repeatedly told by doctors that
he ought not to attempt to live in England, but his father was
failing in body and mind. All disagreement between them
had long ago vanished, and the relationship had become one
of great tenderness. He would not, if he could help it, leave
Britain while his father lived.

He had a surprising impulse to leave it on as mad a wild
goose chase as ever writer imagined. He took, as a rule, very
little interest in politics or in public affairs. " I care nothing
for anything but the moral and the dramatic." Living in a
day when compartments of life still appeared to be water-
tight, he did not find the moral and the dramatic in the
march of contemporary history. His temper was aristocratic.
Easily at home with any individual man who was not too
conventional nor provincial, he despised the opinion of the
majority because they were indifferent to delicacy and
integrity in the arts. He was so much a wanderer that he
really knew almost nothing of ordinary English life, and it
was not until he came to Samoa that he took any interest in
local politics. A sketchy pro-Boer sentiment and a burst of
distress at the death of Gordon, which he said left England
" dripping with blood and daubed with dishonour," seem to
have been his few political emotions until he was roused by
the Curtin affair in the spring of 1887.

The Land League was an associate of Irish tenants pledged
to make life impossible for anybody who accepted the English
rule. A farmer in Kerry, John Curtin, opposed them. They
attacked his farm and killed him. His family resisted, and
drove off the attack, killing one of the raiders, but the
position became untenable, and they had to leave the farm.
Stevenson had always sympathised with the Irish hatred of

English rule and declared that we were to blame for it ; but something in the Curtin story took hold of his imagination. He felt that England had let Gordon down, and was now letting down the Irish who chose to be loyal to her.

He had a horror of men who took the law into their own hands and used such weapons as murder and dynamite. His mind, as his work shows, had been preoccupied during the years at Bournemouth with " that damned old business of the war in the members," which for him meant the uprush of hidden evil and violence against reason and order. It is possible that he externalised this conflict into the Curtin story. This would account for his inexplicable feeling that it was for him to take action.

He proposed to go and live on the farm from which the widow and children of John Curtin had been driven. The devoted Fanny was willing to go with him. Lloyd Osbourne has recorded his own very natural unwillingness to court death on a derelict Irish farm in a cause to which he was completely indifferent, but he seems to have acquiesced.

Stevenson thought that if they were all killed, there would be enough publicity to drive the Government into protecting the Curtins and others in the same position. He also thought that the publicity which his death would cause in America would have some effect on the people there who were financing the rebels. In a long letter to Mrs. Fleeming Jenkin, weighing the pros and cons, he added several other reasons, as that, " Nobody else is taking up this obvious crying duty." " I may die at any moment, my life is of no purchase to an insurance office, it is the less account to husband it, and the business of husbanding life is dreary and demoralising." He considered and dismissed the objections which he had foreseen, that he might be impelled by a wish for excitement, or a thirst for glory, and he adds solemnly in the list of reasons against the enterprise, " The Curtin women are probably thoroughly uninteresting females." The whole letter is a curious document. Did he really mean to go ? Was he striking an attitude in his own mind ? Was he sick of Bournemouth and perhaps temporarily of life ? Lloyd Osbourne thinks that he was influenced by Tolstoy, his passion of the moment, into a crazy desire for sacrifice. Did his novelist mind see the adventure like a story which he longed to implement ? Was he trying to work out some expiation for rebellion in his own life ? Anyhow he did not go. He was summoned instead to Edinburgh to his dying father. The curious emotion over the remote Curtins vanished at once before a real sorrow that went to his very roots. When he arrived in Edinburgh on May 7, Thomas Stevenson, though still on his feet, did not know his son. The next day he died. A friend of the Stevensons, the Reverend D. Robertson, who came to the funeral, still looked upon Louis only as the scapegrace son who had been such an anxiety to his good parents, and gazed with sympathy at his spare figure, pale cheeks, downcast eyes and forlorn look, all of which he attributed to remorse. There was probably a good deal of this in the sorrow which sent him to bed ill for three weeks in Edinburgh, and made the next three months at Skerryvore a period of black depression. Colvin, going once to find him in the garden, says that, " he turned upon me a face that I never saw on him save that once—a face of utter despondency, nay, tragedy, upon which seemed stamped for one concentrated moment the expression of all he had ever had or might yet have to suffer and renounce. Such a countenance was not to be accosted, and I left him."

There was no longer anything to keep Stevenson in Britain.

His mother was willing to join him and go with them wherever the doctors thought best for him. They suggested a hill station in India or Colorado. The idea of going back to America softened for Fanny the blow of leaving Skerryvore, their first real home in which, in spite of her anxiety for Louis, she had been very happy. America it was to be, and the party of five—Stevenson, Fanny, Lloyd Osbourne, the elder Mrs. Stevenson, and Fanny's invaluable French maid, Valentine Roch—booked passages on board the *Ludgate Hill*, which they afterwards discovered to be a cattle ship. There was a farewell party in London, at which Henley, Colvin and other friends found Stevenson " hilariously gay." He was glad to be on the move again and probably was both experiencing a reaction and hiding in his own way his grief at leaving his friends.

Colvin alone was there to say goodbye before the gangway was drawn up and the water widened between Tilbury Dock and the *Ludgate Hill*, which was bearing Stevenson away to fresh wanderings and a new, strange home ; to a blissful spell of comparative health and activity ; to *The Master of Ballantrae* and *Weir of Hermiston* and a South Sea Island grave.

CHAPTER XII

AMERICAN WINTER

IT was eight years since the Amateur Emigrant had sailed for America in search of a wife and of fortune. Now that both of these were his, he sailed for his life. The passage was rough, the ship, which took on board at Havre a cargo of horses, apes and matches, was extremely uncomfortable, but the voyage was one of Stevenson's rare holidays. He was on the move again : he had a case of champagne, a parting present from Henry James, and he enjoyed himself wildly, revelling in a taste of outdoor life in the company of men of action. " Oh, it was lovely in our stable ship chock full of stallions ! " he wrote to Colvin, and to his cousin Bob, " I was so happy on board that ship I could not have believed it possible ! We had the beastliest weather and many discomforts, but the mere fact of it being a tramp ship gave as many comforts ; we would cut about with the men and officers, stay in the wheelhouse, discuss all manner of things, and really be a little at sea. And truly there is nothing else ! I had literally forgotten what happiness was and the full mind, full of external and physical things, not full of cares and rot about a fellow's behaviour. My heart literally sang : I truly care for nothing so much as that."

On arriving at New York he found himself a famous author. Even the two pilots who steered the ships into the harbour were known as Jekyll and Hyde. *Treasure Island*, *Kidnapped*, and even more, *Dr. Jekyll and Mr. Hyde*, had made a greater sensation in America than in England. Reporters were on the quay waiting to interview him. Publishers and editors clamoured for anything he cared to write. A dramatised version of *Dr. Jekyll and Mr. Hyde* was running at one of the Broadway theatres. It was all very different from that first day in New York eight years ago when he tramped the wet streets in a vain search for work. This time he " nearly died of interviews and reporters," and after twenty-four hours " cut for Newport " where he collapsed into bed. Scribners commissioned twelve articles from him at a fee which staggered him. He was elated, but also frightened at the thought of working to order, and he was hankering after the sea again. " I know a little about fame now, and it is nothing compared to a yacht ! " He went to Saranac Lake, high up in the Adirondack Mountains, and took a house there, " in the eye of many winds, with a view of a piece of running water—Highland, all but the dear hue of peat—and of many hills—Highland also but for the lack of heather." Already he sounds the note of homesickness which was to run through his life to the end.

The strong Puritan streak in him made him distrustful of his success. "I had some experience of American appreciation. I liked a little of it, but there is too much ; a little of that would go a long way to spoil a man. I think I began to like it too well. But let us trust the gods ; they have a rod in pickle." Of his contract with Scribners he wrote to William Archer, " I am like to be a millionaire if this goes on, and be publicly hanged at the social revolution ; well, I would prefer that to dying in my bed ; and it would be a godsend to my biographer if I ever have one." People who say such things seldom mean them, but Stevenson always appreciated the dramatic in his own life. He was a story to himself, and no doubt, in theory anyhow, he would like the story to have a good climax.

In the remote surroundings at Saranac, where even the village ink was not meant to write with, he was far enough away from literary lionising. His health improved, and he began serious work again. " I have fallen head over heels into a new tale, *The Master of Ballantrae*. ' Come,' said I to my engine, ' let us make a tale, a story of many years and countries, of the sea and the land, savagery and civilisation.' . . . I need not tell my brothers of the craft that I was in the most interesting moments of an author's life. The hours that followed, whether walking abroad or lying wakeful in bed, were hours of unadulterated joy." In that " ' Come,' said I to my engine," lies a great deal of Stevenson's method, the secret perhaps both of his failures and his success. He wrote too much by will. His will was strong, he wound and wound at his engine and never failed to draw up some water out of the well, but the deepest water did not always rise.

Lloyd Osbourne was also writing. He was at work on the first draft of *The Wrong Box*, in which Stevenson later collaborated, though it seems likely from all evidence that his share in it was not great. It is an ingenious mock-gruesome mystery story about a corpse that is substituted for a statue in a case : a *tour de force* sometimes enlivened by a faintly ghoulish humour, but with no breath of reality in the characters.

Stevenson's volume of verse, *Underwoods*, was published in England just after he sailed for America. He was not a born poet. He could not bear not to have a try at anything, and just as he had tried to write plays, so he tried to write poetry, achieving a good deal of verse, sometimes happy, occasionally striking, often just bad, but interesting to his friends and admirers because it epitomised his philosophy, and bore the authentic note of his personality. Prose was his medium. There is far more poetry in *Weir of Hermiston* than in any of the rhymes he ever wrote, it has the magic that is missing from his verse. In some ways he wrote prose as a poet writes poetry ; no man ever searched more meticulously for the image word, but if he sometimes wrote prose like a poet, he often wrote poetry like a prose writer. He had no wings.

The poems are particularly interesting to any student of Stevenson's style, because they show perhaps even more clearly than his prose the kind of words that he liked to use most often. He used a great many monosyllables, and especially those adjectives which call up an image of fine weather, of daylight and distance. " Bright," " airy," " clear," " fair." " Bright " and " fair " are words never far from his pen. The child who was so often lonely and ill in the misty grey Edinburgh winter must very early have associated happiness with the summer days at Colinton, when he could play out of doors with the other children. He had suffered in his childhood from night terrors and feverish wakefulness, so that daylight must have meant a release to him. All his life Stevenson loved countries, such as the shores of his beloved Mediterranean, where the sun was bright and the light was clear. There is, too, about all his writing, prose or poetry, the lucent colour of a dream. " Bright is the ring of words," is both an example and a summary of his style. The beginnings of his short stories and novels often suggest somebody going out of doors for the first time on a fine morning.

Underwoods contained some of his best-known verses, "Requiem," " A House Beautiful," " The Celestial Surgeon," " Our Lady of the Snows," " It is not yours—oh mother, to complain." It also contains the lines in which he links his own life work with the work of his engineering forefather, and apologises to his father probably for his desertion.

> Say not of me that weakly I declined
> The labours of my sires, and fled the sea,
> The towers we founded, and the lamps we lit
> To play at home with paper like a child,
> But rather say, "In the afternoon of time
> A strenuous family dusted from its hands
> The sand of granite, and beholding far
> Along the sandy coast its pyramids
> And tall memorials catch the dying sun
> Smiled well content, and to this childish task
> Around the fire addressed its evening hours."

Memories and Portraits, the second volume of Stevenson's collected essays, was published in England while he was at Saranac. It contains many of his most characteristic essays: *Talk and Talkers*; *A Humble Remonstrance*, the article on the Art of Fiction addressed to Henry James and already quoted. It includes the *Gossip on Romance* and the very characteristic *A Penny Plain and Twopence Coloured* in which he goes back to the Toy Theatre of his childhood, to that coloured world of fantasy and romantic adventure which was in the marrow of his bones. It also includes a memoir of his father, published within a month of his death. With tender pride he wrote his father's epitaph. "The result of his work was that in all parts of the world a safer landfall awaits the mariner." It was in comparison with such a solid achievement that Louis Stevenson felt his own work to be a childish task, a culmination of the child's game of make-believe which he had played around the chairs and sofas at home, perhaps in the room where his father was busy with the plans that were to save so many lives.

In the meantime he worked at his monthly series of articles for *Scribners*, the first being *A Chapter on Dreams*. When he wrote it, Freud, who was six years younger than Stevenson, was only at the beginning of his discoveries and had as yet published nothing. Almost any average reader of to-day could, up to a point, interpret the dream about the son who returned from abroad to find his father married again, murdered his father, and lived on with his stepmother until his terror that she might discover and disclose his crime was resolved by her confession that she loved him. Stevenson had no idea how much of himself he was giving away, nor how far the dream explained the remorse which always coloured his feelings for his father, for after all, in thinking differently from his parents, breaking away from home and marrying when he pleased, he had done no more than a man should. The second half of the essay is a vivid and interesting account of the part played by his unconscious mind, his " Brownies," in his creative work.

The second of the *Scribners* essays was *The Lantern Bearers*, in which a boy's glee in a dark lantern, which can serve no possible purpose except to please him, is the stepping-stone for a discussion on romance and realism. The other essays include, *Pulvis et Umbra*, a piece of rather grandiose moralising ; *Beggars* and *Christmas Sermon* and the admirable *Letter to a Young Gentleman who Proposes to Embrace the Career of Art*, which has already been quoted. Whether about life or letters, Stevenson loved to preach, and knew that he loved it. He had an overwhelming desire to pass on to other people his strong convictions about how to write and how to live.

In spite of his dislike for cold climates, the winter at
Saranac was happy and productive, but the rod which the
gods had in pickle was a violent quarrel with Henley. There
had been difficulties in their relationship for some time, the
chief of them that Henley did not like Fanny and she did
not like him, feeling that he exhausted her husband by his
flow of talk, and took up too much of his time with schemes
for collaboration that could never be successful. No doubt
there was jealousy on both sides. Without knowing it they
competed for Louis; Fanny won. The failure of their
plays had been a far greater disappointment to Henley than
to Stevenson. Perhaps, too, he had felt nearer to the
struggling author than to the writer for whom recognition
and success were opening. The final breach came suddenly.
Henley wrote a letter to Louis accusing Fanny of plagiarising
an unpublished story by a friend of both, Mrs. Katherine
de Mattos. Stevenson wrote back at once on a note of
hysterical rage. They were thousands of miles apart. It
was not as though they could have a flaming quarrel and get
over it. Each wrote things that the other could not forgive.
Stevenson was miserable, the more so as he had other feelings
beside rage. " Lord, I can't help loving the man," he wrote
after abusing Henley. " I know his merit, damn him."
The quarrel took the heart out of him and made life seem a
nightmare. He longed to be at sea again, away from letters
and in that relaxation of the nerves which he only seemed
able to enjoy on board ship. Fanny went to San Francisco
to look for a yacht, found the *Casco*, a boat of 74 tons, wired
to Louis for his consent and bought it. The family set sail
again from San Francisco on September 28th, to cruise
around the South Sea Islands.

CHAPTER XIII

" THE MASTER OF BALLANTRAE "

STEVENSON spent the next eighteen months at sea, or calling at the Pacific Islands, with a longer pause at Honolulu, where he finished *The Master of Ballantrae* and *The Wrong Box*. His health improved more than anybody had dared to hope. He was able to lead an ordinary life, "sea bathing and cutting about the world loose, like a grown-up person." His plan was to write a book about the South Sea Islands, and partly for this reason and partly from his natural delight in active experience after his years of bed, he courted every adventure. He drank champagne with the last of the Hawaian kings. He spent a week in the leper settlement where Father Damien worked, and played croquet with the leper children, sending an appeal through Colvin for bits of material, dressmakers' snippings, with which the little girls in the settlement could make dolls' clothes. He was stranded on the island of Tautira, waiting for the yacht to come back with stores, and took the oath of brotherhood with the Chief, Ori a Ori. "The interest," Stevenson wrote to Colvin, "has been incredible." On a night "warm as milk," under a blanket in the cockpit with the southern stars above him, his mind went back to the early days in Edinburgh. "I remember all I hoped and feared as I pickled about in the rain and east wind. I feared I should make a mere shipwreck and yet timidly hoped not. I feared I should never have a friend, far less a wife, and yet passionately hoped I might ; how I hoped (if I did not take to drink) I should possibly write one little book, and then—now what a change ! I feel somehow as if I should like the incident set upon a brass plate at the corner of that dreary thoroughfare for all students to read, poor devils, when their hearts are down."

Imprisoned in his room at Davos and Bournemouth he had found change and adventure in his writing. It was not so easy to settle down to a half-finished novel in a world which was like his most romantic tale, but he had to earn the family's living. The first parts of *The Master of Ballantrae* were already appearing in *Scribners*, and Stevenson drove himself to write the end. "The hardest job I ever had to do," he remarked. "It contains more human work than anything of mine except *Kidnapped*."

It has been said that every novelist only writes one fundamental story. Certainly *The Master of Ballantrae* has the same essential theme as *Dr. Jekyll and Mr. Hyde*. Again the decent man and the bad man are linked together, this time not as two souls in one body, but as sons of the same father. Again good is overpowered by evil until the kindly, honourable Henry Durie draws his sword upon his brother, and is finally so swamped by hatred that he becomes insane and stoops to plot his death. The story, narrated by Ephraim Mackellar, the loyal, priggish, selfless servant of the house of Durrisdeer, is always sober and often sombre in tone. There is little colour and no relief ; Alison's beauty, the old Lord's courteous dignity, are the stimulus to rivalry between the two brothers. The young children of the house are objects of contention. Spirit and charm belong only to the devil, to the Master of Ballantrae, who uses them to shatter the happiness of his father's house, and whose very existence threatens his brother's peace, even from the other side of the world.

The early chapters about the relationships of the family at Durrisdeer are some of Stevenson's best work. It is true

that Alison, probable as all her reactions are, never comes to
life.   She must of necessity be seen from outside, since
Ephraim Mackellar tells the story, but even so she does not
live and breathe as the men do.   Stevenson, as he knew,
could not yet draw a woman, but the reader feels Henry's
unhappiness, even when he finds it difficult to care very much
about Henry, who is, it must be confessed, a dull dog.   The
reader feels, too, the evil charm of the Master, so potent that
even in the long years of absence he holds sway in the hearts
of his father and of the woman who loved him, but became his
brother's wife.   The story flags when the Chevalier Burke
appears, and we have to wade through his account of the
Master's wanderings.   This part of the work is a tiresome
interruption, part of an indifferent boys' story.   Its only
value is to emphasise the bitter resentment which the Master
felt for his sufferings, and his callous brutality on every
occasion.   These could perhaps have been conveyed without
the skull-and-crossbones interlude.   The interest only
quickens again when the Master is back at Durrisdeer working
out his revenge on the brother who supplanted him.   The
play of feeling between the four in the house is most skilfully
handled, till tension mounts to a climax, and Henry Durie,
the gentle and good, strikes his brother and takes down a
pair of naked swords from the wall.   Mackellar, who has
stood so nobly by his employer and whose moral courage is
so unswerving, fails him at this point for sheer lack of
physical courage.   When the Master turns his blade upon
him and the light runs along the steel, his protests fade from his
lips.   Trembling and ashamed, he takes up the candles, and
goes before them into the black night where " a windless
stricture of frost bound the air," to act as second to the
monstrous duel.   It comes as something of a surprise that

Henry should be too much for the Master, but the whole of the scene with its horror—horror that, like the first scene in *Hamlet*, seems intensified by the cold and the midnight hour—and its phantasmagoric ending is told with an economy and power that equal anything Stevenson wrote. The primeval curse is upon the house of Durrisdeer. Henry, in intent if not in effect, has committed the sin of Cain and from that hour begins his slow deterioration.

It must be admitted that the novel also deteriorates, and especially after the introduction of the Indian, Secundra Dass, who may be based on fact, but is never artistically convincing. Stevenson's imagination was caught by the story of an Indian fakir who was able to bury a man and then bring him back to life. He transplanted this to a North American setting and used it for the end of *The Master of Ballantrae*. Whether it is that East is East and West is West and never the twain shall meet, or whether Stevenson was interrupted in his work by that pleasure in living which had so long been denied him, or whether just that he never could end as well as he began, *The Master of Ballantrae* tails off, in spite of the careful craftsmanship of a man whose technique was at his finger-tips.

Opinions were divided about it ; Henry James thought highly of it, but some of Stevenson's usual admirers, Henley and Leslie Stephen, complained of it as " grim " and " grimy," and were displeased because the good man was not more attractive.

On a visit to Sydney in 1890, Stevenson made another of his sudden and impassioned dives into public affairs. He saw printed in a Sydney newspaper a letter in which a Dr. Hyde, a missionary living in Honolulu, had launched an attack against Father Damien who had organised the leper settlement which Stevenson had visited. Father Damien was, Hyde said, a coarse, dirty man, headstrong and bigoted. Stevenson, in a letter to *The Times*, defended Damien and attacked Hyde. He admitted that Damien had faults, and had made a hash of running the settlement, but pointed out that " by a striking act of martyrdom, he directed all eyes to that distressful country. The man who did what Damien did is my father and the father of all who love goodness." Stevenson attacked Hyde because he had never even been to the leper island. He knew that he risked a libel action in launching this attack, but Hyde only dismissed him as " a cranky Bohemian." It is interesting that the name of the man who provoked this violent denunciation was Hyde and that he roused Stevenson's fury by attacking a man whom he called father. Was the Dr. Jekyll in Stevenson attacking his own baser half ?

Stevenson's plan was to go back to England for the summer by way of Australia, but a sharp illness and hæmorrhage in Sydney made it clear that, unlike most consumptives, he could only live in the tropics. He was obliged to go to sea again to recover. He knew now that he would never realise his dream of rattling in a cab through the lights of London to Colvin's door. " I must tell you plainly," he wrote to Henry James, " I can't tell Colvin. I do not think I shall come to England more than once and that will be to die." He adds, " These last two years I have been much at sea and have never wearied, never once did I lose my fidelity to the blue water and a ship. It is plain that for me my exile to the place of schooners and islands can be in no sense regarded as a calamity." There was another side of it for the man who wrote " Be it granted me to behold you again in dying, hills of home," but it was not his philosophy nor his habit to emphasise his losses. He looked about for somewhere in the South Sea islands to make a permanent home. In the islands of Samoa he had written his first South Sea story—*The Bottle Imp*. The climate suited him, and there was one great advantage, that Samoa was connected by a monthly post with San Francisco, so that it would be possible for him to keep in touch with his publishers and with civilisation. He was half-way through both *The Wrecker* and *The Ebb Tide*, then called *The Pearl Fishers*, and was writing a good deal of verse. He needed to settle down and get on with the work in hand. Lloyd Osbourne went back to England to wind up the family affairs there. The elder Mrs. Stevenson had already returned to Scotland, though later she was to rejoin her son at Vailima. Louis and Fanny went to Samoa, and as they had done in so many other places set about making a home.

CHAPTER XIV

SAMOA

THE islands of the Samoan group were under the triple control of England, America and Germany. This had been established a few months before Stevenson came to live there, at the Berlin Convention of July 1889. The same Convention had deposed the King, Mataafa, whose rule had been vigorous and popular, but who had been rash enough to defeat a handful of German troops in a skirmish. The Convention replaced Mataafa with a cousin of his, Maelita Laupepa. In Stevenson's opinion Laupepa, whose claim was no better than Mataafa's, was far less fit to rule. Later events were to confirm this, but in the meantime Mataafa, allowed no share in the government, withdrew to something between a palace and a camp outside the town of Apia, and lived there, a King-Over-the-Water on dry land, uncomfortably near to his successful rival. At the time when Stevenson came to Samoa, Laupepa and Mataafa were outwardly on friendly terms, but Mataafa's household was a lively focus for discontent. Here were the Jacobites of Stevenson's novels, within a few miles of his house. No wonder he immediately embroiled himself.

He was the more tempted to do so because the two white men appointed by the Berlin Convention as Chief Justice and President, a Swede and a German, were hopelessly unequal to their task. They were weak when they should have been firm, and harsh instead of just, inflexible when tact was needed. They alienated everybody on the island, black and white. The Consuls of the three controlling nations were supposed to act as an official board of advisers to the King, but they could not, and did not, achieve much in the general welter of interests.

As soon as he grasped the situation, Stevenson set out to do two things, to reconcile Mataafa and Laupepa, and to get the German nominees removed from the government of the island. He never managed the first. In 1893 open war broke out between the King *de facto* and the King *de iure*. Mataafa was beaten and driven into exile. His second object Stevenson did achieve. By a series of letters to *The Times*, which *The Time*, backed with a leader, he drew attention to the mismanagement under which the Samoans were suffering. He was in danger at one time of being deported from the island, where German influence was predominant, but he continued his outcries and won his point. There was an inquiry, and the Chief Justice and President were replaced in 1893 by better men. After Stevenson's death in 1894 the Germans swung round and supported Mataafa. The Samoan affairs were muddled along between the three countries to the great discomfort of the inhabitants, until 1899, when England withdrew her claims altogether, America took the island of Tutuila, with the best harbour, and Germany remained in sole possession of the larger islands. After 1905 the house at Vailima which Stevenson built became the Government House, first for German and then for English governors of the island.

This was the political background to the last years of Stevenson's life. It engaged so much of his attention that Colvin, to whom he wrote a monthly diary letter, trembled for his literary work. He thought these affairs were " exasperatingly petty and obscure, however grave the potential European complications which lay behind them " ;

6

it is clear that the scholar of the British Museum, though he never failed in his loyalty to his friend, was disconcerted by the new Stevenson, who spent days in the saddle and in an open boat and was ardently involved in the strange doings of black kings. Stevenson had borne the invalid years bravely, and his friends did not perhaps realise how much he had hated the confined life, nor how far he was from being only a writer. " Our civilisation is a dingy business, it leaves so much out of a man." Physical adventures and hardships had been some of the things left out of his life. Samoa gave him a taste of them in his last years, and the experience was sharpened by contrast. He had written so much, and in some ways lived so little. What wonder if he wanted to live almost more than to write ? In London they thought of him as a forlorn exile. He was often homesick, he would have liked to go back and see them, but he was certainly not weeping by the waters of Babylon.

It was not always local politics that absorbed him in those first months at Vailima. He was for the first time a landowner and his house was growing before his eyes. In December 1890, he wrote to his American publisher, " By autumn we hope to be sprawling in our verandah, twelve feet, sir, by eight in front, and seven and a half on the flank ; view of the sea and mountains, sunrise, and the German fleet at anchor three miles away in Apia harbour. I know a hedge where the lemons grow. My house at the moment smells of them strongly ; and the rain which a while ago roared there, now rings in minute drops upon the iron roof : I have no *Wrecker* for you this mail, other things having engaged me."

He goes on to talk of the other things. " I am a mere farmer : my talk, which would scarce interest you on

Broadway, is all of fuafua and tui tui and black boys, and planting and weeding and axes and cutlasses ; my hands are covered with blisters ; letters are doubtless a fine thing, so are beer and skittles, but give me farming in the tropics for real interest. Life goes in enchantment : I come home to find I am late for dinner, and when I go to bed I could cry for the weariness of my loins and thighs. Do not speak to me of vexation, this life brims with it, but with living interest fairly." It was probably an exasperating letter for the publisher who was waiting for *The Wrecker*, and could not care about the weeds, but it sings with the exultation of a prisoner restored to life.

In the meantime he toiled on with his deplorably dull book about the South Seas, which appeared serially in *Black and White* in 1891, and was published as a book after his death. What streak of perversity in him made this, which might have been a sparkling chronicle of adventures and delights, a mere tedium to the reader ? Fanny, nearly always right about his work, had seen while they were still cruising around the islands, that he was going the wrong way about it. " Louis has," she wrote to Colvin, " the most enchanting material that anyone ever had in the world for his book, and I am afraid he is going to spoil it all. He has taken into his Scotch Stevenson head that a stern duty lies before him and that his book must be a sort of scientific and historical impersonal thing, comparing the different languages (of which he knows nothing really) and the different peoples, the object being to settle the question as to whether they are of common Malay origin or not. Also to compare the Protestant and Catholic missionaries, etc., and the whole thing is to be impersonal, leaving out all he knows of the people themselves. And I believe there is no one living who has got so near them and understands them as he does ! Louis says it is a stern duty that is at the bottom of it, which is more alarming than anything else ! He may in this conscientious state of mind—and I think he has—put nothing in his diary but statistics ! "

Perhaps to Stevenson this labour took the place of that history of the Highlands of Scotland which he had so fortunately broken off to write *Treasure Island*. Perhaps his life was at the moment so full of colour that he needed a work of sober reality to pin it down. Anyhow he missed his chance, and few even of his most devoted admirers want to labour more than once, if that, through his book on the South Seas.

If *The Wrecker* was no *Treasure Island* to ravish him away from statistics, it was at least not dull. He managed to finish it in the autumn of 1892, nearly a year after he first came to Samoa to settle. He had begun it in collaboration with Lloyd Osbourne, but finished it alone while Lloyd Osbourne was in England. The early chapters, Loudon Dodd's life in artists' circles in Paris, recall Stevenson's own youth there, the days of irresponsible freedom and happiness with his cousin Bob, described half-laughingly but with the nostalgic tenderness of a man for his boyhood ; though Loudon Dodd has nothing of Stevenson's underlying purpose, only a general taste for the arts, without the vocation to make him an artist. He, too—how the *leit-motiv* recurs— is a son who has chosen his own life in opposition to his father's wishes. He is a desultory figure, who allows himself to be directed by his more positive friend, Jim Pinkerton, a man to whom money-making is all that art was not to Loudon Dodd—a passion, a preoccupation, a binding claim. Pinkerton in his own line is the real artist, the game matters to him more than the rewards, he lives and sleeps speculation, and in his ingenuous concentration and his affectionate loyalty to his friend, he remains an endearing figure. Pinkerton slips into the background after the auction scene, in which Loudon Dodd, gambling wildly on an unknown value for which others are making fantastic bids, wins a wrecked schooner stranded on a coral island, and goes off to redeem his prize. From that point *The Wrecker* is a mystery story in which the mystery is well kept. Stevenson was greatly relieved when it was finished, but, instead of the rest he had been looking forward to, he began almost at once on a new story, called at that time *The Highlands of Upolu,* but later *The Beach of Falesá.*

The idea of *The Beach of Falesá* " shot through me like a bullet," he said, but he did not finish it until September of the next year, 1892. He thought it one of the best things he had done : " It is the first realistic South Sea story. I mean with real South Sea characters, and details of life. . . . I have got the smell and look of the thing a good deal ; you will know more of the South Seas after you have read my little tale than if you had read a library." The story, told in the first person by Wiltshire, the trader, is both admirably exciting and a comment on the relationship between white man and black in the islands, a tract which contains no moralising. It contains also a key to his own excellent relationship with the Samoans and with all the South Sea Islanders. " It's easy to find out what Kanakas think," Wiltshire remarks. " Just go back to yourself any way round from ten to fifteen years old, and there is an average Kanaka." Going back to himself at any age was always easy for Stevenson.

In this year he also began *A Footnote to History,* his account

of the troubles in Samoa. Some of his friends were distressed
that he should identify himself so completely with his adopted
community. To others he was becoming a legend, a white
writer living among savages in scenes of tropical beauty.
" Since Byron was in Greece," Edmund Gosse wrote to
him, " nothing has appealed to the ordinary literary man so
much as that you should be living in the South Seas." He
still hoped, as he wrote to Henry James, to come back to
Europe and spend the summer in the South of France, where
his friends might visit him, but there was not much conviction
behind this hope. In spite of the new life and the crowding
occupations, he was now working as hard as ever. He
found *A Footnote to History* a toil, but his ardent sympathy
for the Samoans made him look on it as a duty. " How do
journalists fetch up their drivel ! " he wrote to Colvin. " I
aim at only clearness and the most obvious finish . . . and
yet it has taken me two months to write 45,000 words. . . .
After that I'll have a spank at fiction."

CHAPTER XV

"CATRIONA"

THE spank at fiction was *Catriona*, the sequel to *Kidnapped*, at first known as *David Balfour*. Stevenson was playing with the idea of a novel called *Sophia Scarlet*, about three young ladies who came out from their English school to the plantations. It was one of those false starts which novelists so often make and of which he was especially prolific. One night when he was awake with colic and trying to finish the *Footnote to History* the real novel broke through. "I slid off into *David Balfour*, some fifty pages of which are drafted and like me well!" "*David*," he said, had been kept hanging about for five years at the door of the British Linen Company's Bank of Edinburgh, but "he still has a kick in his shanks." "The tale interferes with my eating and sleeping." He worked at it steadily with very few checks, and finished it in four months.

The pace was the more surprising because his life was so full. His household had grown, his mother was with him again, Lloyd Osbourne back from England, and his step-daughter, Belle, with her twelve-year-old son, Austin, came to pay them a long visit. Stevenson added to his other functions that of tutor, giving the boy lessons in history and English. An unknown cousin, Graham Balfour, came out to stay with them, became a close friend of Stevenson, and was later to write his life, that first biography of a dead author, which, as so often, contains a great deal of invaluable material but is inhibited by too much personal feeling and consideration for the family.

Stevenson's household also included a dozen native servants in whom he was much interested as he was in the problems and difficulties of all Samoans. He had become the Chieftain of the Clan, and even, to please his mother, conducted family prayers for the whole household. This gave him a new chance to experiment, and he wrote the well-known " Vailima Prayers," of which Andrew Lang remarked unkindly, but with some truth, that he was " graciously presenting the Deity with specimens of his literary skill." At least the prayers expressed Stevenson's simple nursery morality. " The day," he informed God, " returns and brings us the petty round of irritating concerns and duties. Help us to play the man, help us to perform them with laughter and kind faces, let cheerfulness abound with industry, give us to go blithely about our business all this day, bring us to our resting beds weary and content and undishonoured and grant us in the end the gift of sleep."

Besides his other occupations there was an endless exchange of hospitality with the inhabitants of the island, both brown and white. In the meantime the quarrel between Mataafa and Laupepa was blowing up, and the German threat of deportation was drawing nearer to the meddling British novelist, though this only seems to have amused him. No wonder Colvin trembled for his friend's literary work as he waded his way through the endless dissertations on Samoan politics. " You are to understand that if I take all this bother it is not for a sense of duty or love of meddling, but for the great affection I have for Mataafa, a dear, sweet old fellow." Stevenson's feelings were, as Henry James said, his reasons. But *David Balfour* went " skelping along." It was too old and too deeply-rooted a purpose in life to be shaken, and there was the family living to earn. Every morning from six to eleven, even the cause of the wronged and entrancing Mataafa was in the background, and Stevenson trod the streets of Edinburgh in the respectable shape of David Balfour, who would certainly have thought the Samoans uncivilised.

The central theme of *Catriona* is the trial of James Stewart of the Glens for the murder of Colin Campbell. David had glimpsed the murderer just enough to be certain that it was not James, and he feels it to be his duty to go to Inveraray and give evidence. Everybody in the book except David knows that at the trial of a Stewart in the Campbell head-quarters before a Campbell jury, a bit of evidence is neither here nor there. Everybody knows, too, that if James of the Glens is innocent of this crime, it was only for lack of courage and opportunity. David, that born civil servant, has a deep-rooted respect for law and order, and the objective fact. Anyhow he must do what is right out of respect for himself, for he soon discovers that James is not worthy of much respect. His conscience is reinforced, he falls in love with James' daughter Catriona, beautiful, trustful, innocent, and devoted to her rascally father. David is kidnapped again and swept off to the Bass Rock, where he hears the superb " Tale of Todd Lapraik," a ghost story that rivals *Thrawn Janet*, an irrelevance in the novel *Catriona* which even a purist could hardly regret. By sheer force of persistence David gets to Inveraray to find that the trial is over and that James is convicted.

It is a shock to David, still unsuspicious of tortuous ways, to find James' escape connived at by the authorities, and still more to find himself with Catriona on the same ship bound for Holland and to discover that her father, who promised to meet her there, has not turned up at the rendezvous, and the girl, alone and helpless in a strange country, is left to the protection of David. Needless to say he stands by her nobly, and respects her virtue, while her father, when he does arrive, simply does not believe in such unnecessary self-denial, and cheerfully proceeds to sponge on David. But David has never been the man to allow himself to be victimised, and he deals so firmly with James that he loses both him and Catriona. Alan Breck Stewart, whose occasional reappearances warm and colour the pages, brings the story to a happy ending.

Except for the insubstantial *Otto*, *Catriona* is the first of Stevenson's novels to include two women among the important characters. True they are both drawn from outside and superficially at that. Barbara Grant is not much more than a pleasant, chaffing manner. Catriona is certainly more alive than Alison in *The Master of Ballantrae*, but she is, as Stevenson himself remarked, " as virginal as billy oh ! "— more child than girl. It is difficult to believe that any young woman living alone with David in the rooms at Leyden could be so completely unaware of his difficulties, and so puzzled by the distance that the conscientious young man insisted on setting between them. Christina, of *Weir of Hermiston*, a really feminine creature, would have known more than that in her cradle.

Stevenson remarked with pride that now that he was so old—as soon as he had turned forty he appeared to himself to be senile—he was beginning to write about women and to write love stories. Why had he been so slow in coming to it ? His own explanation was that his especial gift was for the exact description of physical states, and that he was afraid of " grossness " and also feared to offend against the taboo on sex that inhibited the British novel. He complained bitterly that the French did not allow themselves to be so restricted, but it does not seem probable that he really minded the taboo very much. Exact descriptions of physical states might be prohibited, but an age which produced Catherine Earnshaw, Becky Sharp and Maggie Tulliver was not entirely cut off from female characterisation. In five of Stevenson's novels, *Treasure Island*, *Kidnapped*, *Dr. Jekyll and Mr. Hyde*, *The Wrecker* and *The Ebb Tide*, no woman occurs at all. Not until the two Christinas in *Weir of Hermiston* did he breathe the breath of life into a female character. He suffered from a deep-rooted shyness about love, to which one key may perhaps be found in his revealing chapter on dreams. His early affairs in Edinburgh were probably uneasy, and happy as he undoubtedly was with Fanny, romantic as the circumstances of his courtship were, she may have stood to him for reassurance and for companionship rather than for passion. It is not, after all, natural for a man of twenty-five to marry a woman already a grandmother. He may, too, have suppressed unconsciously the female side of his own nature. A novelist has both male and female in himself to draw on apart from outside experience.

The truth was that in that emotional core from which all fiction springs, Stevenson was always years behind his age. To the end his favourite authors were Scott and Dumas. " It all comes back," Henry James remarked, " to his feeling for the juvenile. Women are almost wholly absent from his pages, for they don't like ships and pistols and fights, they encumber the decks, require separate apartments, and almost worst of all, have not the highest literary standards. Why should a person marry when he might be swinging a cutlass or looking for buried treasure ? " In fact a man may live what appears to be a grown-up life, but his novels betray him. Stevenson took years to work through the comparative safety of adolescence, and only showed the beginning of emotional maturity in that fragment of *Weir of Hermiston* in which a young man who has openly defied his father falls in love with a woman whom he knows that his father would forbid him. At which point Stevenson died.

CHAPTER XVI

THE EDINBURGH EDITION

IN the intervals of other work, Stevenson was writing verse, some of it about the South Seas, some harking back to memories of home. The collection published as *Songs of Travel* were nearly all written in the last six years of his life. These included " Give to me the life I love," " I will make you brooches and toys for your delight," " Bright is the ring of words." The lines written to Fanny, "Trusty, dusky, vivid, true," and the lines to S. R. Crockett, in acknowledgment of a dedication, which expressed his underlying sadness at being cut off from his own country,

> Blows the wind to-day, and the sun and the rain are flying,
> Blows the wind on the moors to-day and now,
> Where above the graves of the martyrs the whaups are crying,
> My heart remembers how.

Stevenson's heart did indeed remember how. The Scotch scenes in *Catriona* and *Weir of Hermiston* have the freshness of something seen yesterday. He saw them as clearly and wrote of them with as certain a touch as he saw and wrote of the tropical scenes before his bodily eyes.

Among his other disabilities he was constantly threatened with writer's cramp, a serious matter in those days before typewriters had come into use, but in spite of this threat and of all his other work, he was an indefatigable letter writer, putting a lot of his energy—especially into the monthly journal to Colvin. He had begun this simply with the idea of keeping in touch, but as time went on it occurred to him that selections of these letters might be worth publishing after his death to make some provision for his wife and stepchildren. He mentioned this to Colvin, who afterwards edited the letters for publication under the title *Vailima Letters*. Later a full edition of his letters was published which included many of those written in earlier life. His letters were among the best things that he ever wrote. There is not one of them that does not bear the stamp of his vivid and stimulating personality, and his running commentary on his own writing and the work of his contemporaries must always be interesting to anybody who cares for the craft.

The character of *Weir of Hermiston* was suggested by the famous judge, Lord Braxfield, whose portrait by Raeburn had fascinated Stevenson as a young man. In October of 1892, a few months after *Catriona*, Stevenson mentioned in a letter to Colvin, " My new novel," and went on to discuss the title and characters of *Weir of Hermiston*, at that time called *The Lord Justice Clerk*. He dropped the idea for a time, as his custom was, and turned to another novel, *The Young Chevalier*, a tale about Prince Charlie in the years after the '45, of which he only wrote a fragment.

The tension in Samoa was heightening. In November he wrote to Colvin, "This is a strange life I live, always on the brink of deportation . . . the new house is roofed, it will be a braw house, and what is better, I have my yearly bill in and find I can pay it. I must have made close on £4000 this year all told ; but what is not so pleasant, I seem to have come near to spending them." While writing *Catriona* he had been in good spirits, but a note of anxiety about money and depression about work now begins to recur in his letters. He had two attacks of influenza that winter. In February

1893, he and Fanny and Belle went to Sydney for a holiday. He enjoyed himself and bought Fanny a " gaudy black velvet dress trimmed with lace," but she was ill there and did not recover at first when they got back to Samoa. For some weeks he was anxious about her. He was at work with Lloyd Osbourne on *The Ebb Tide*, which he finished in May. His comment on it was, "well, up a high hill he heaved a huge round stone." He was pleased with the book, a grim study of shady characters in the South Seas. " I can't think what to say about the tale, but it seems to me to go off with a considerable bang ! In fact to be an extraordinary work ; but whether popular ? Attwater is no end of a courageous attempt. I think you will admit, etc., etc. In short as you see I am a trifle vainglorious. But, O, it has been such a grind ! The devil himself would allow a man to brag a little after such a crucifixion ! I break down at every paragraph and lie here and sweat till I can get one sentence wrung out after another." He was probably tired and needed a longer rest after *Catriona*, but his febrile nature would not let him rest. " No rest but the grave, for Sir Walter. Oh, how that rings in a man's head."

He had hardly finished *The Ebb Tide* before he began his *History of a Family of Engineers*, the story of his grandfather, Robert Stevenson. So his interest swings to and fro between the old and the new, between the flotsam of the South Seas and his Scotch forefathers. As before, he found what rest he was able to take in change of work. " I have left fiction wholly and gone to my grandfather, and on the whole found peace."

In July open war broke out between Mataafa and Laupepa. Stevenson helped to organise a temporary hospital for the wounded. He was excited by the fighting, but distressed at the defeat of Mataafa. The note of depression sounds again in a letter to his old Edinburgh friend, Charles Baxter : " I perceive by a thousand signs that we grow old "—he was forty-three—" and are soon to pass away ; I hope with dignity—if not, with courage at least. I am myself very ready and would be—will be—when I have made a little money for my folks. It is strange, I must seem to you to blaze in a Birmingham prosperity and happiness, and to myself I seem a failure. The truth is, I have never got over the last influenza yet and am miserably out of heart." He worked steadily on at his family records, but felt incapable of fiction—hardly surprising, since he had finished two novels in the last eighteen months ; but the incapacity distressed him. Perhaps there was somewhere in him the knowledge that he was racing against time.

In spite of another illness and of his inability for fiction, he started at the New Year a fresh novel, *St. Ives,* a lively mannered adventure story of the escape of a French prisoner in the Napoleonic wars from Edinburgh Castle. He wrote of it with some despondency, " my work goes along but slowly, I have got to a crossing place I suppose, the present book *St. Ives* is nothing. It is in no style in particular, a tissue of adventures, the central character not very well done, no philosophic pith under the yarn—I like doing it though, and if you ask me why ! " That he liked doing it is probably the reason why *St. Ives,* although his own criticism is true, has a certain panache, and is very readable. He left it unfinished and Quiller-Couch added the last few chapters.

Two great pleasures came to him in this last year of his life, one from the old world and one from the new. Charles Baxter was able to arrange with Chatto and Windus for the first collected edition of Stevenson's works, the Edinburgh

Edition, suggested to Baxter by a dream in which he saw a whole shelf full of books by Stevenson bound like the old Edinburgh Edition of Scott. The collected edition should have been a good offset to Stevenson's feelings that he was a failure, and would make a great difference to the position in which he would leave his family if he were to die soon. His friends were surprised and hurt that he was not more elated, but he was tired and dispirited and felt that he had written himself out. A little later he revived and took a more natural pleasure in the solid laurel wreath. He probably felt that if his creative power was failing there was not much satisfaction in republications of his work, and he was altogether out of heart. Lloyd Osbourne records that he often missed Stevenson in the evening, and found that he had stolen out alone and was gazing sadly up at the summit of Mount Vaea, where he had decided that he should be buried. One volume of the Edinburgh Edition reached Samoa before he died.

He rejoiced much more fully in the other pleasure that came to him. He had now lived for three years in Samoa and was beloved by its people. He had championed their cause to some effect, acted as umpire in their disputes and advised in their problems, showing them much affection. There was no road up to his house. It was necessary to bring everything up on pack-horses by a narrow path through the undergrowth. On the 2nd of September of this year a deputation of Samoan chiefs came to see him and told him that they were going to make him a road connecting his house with the public way. There was to be no question of payment, it was to be a token of gratitude from the political prisoners whom he had befriended. It was to be known as the Road of the Loving Heart, a free gift to Tusitala, Teller of Tales. In a month the road was finished. A board was set up bearing in Samoan this inscription :

THE ROAD OF GRATITUDE.

Considering the great love of His Excellency Tusitala in his loving care of us in our tribulation in the prison. We have prepared this splendid gift. It shall never be muddy, it shall endure for ever, this road that we have made.

Stevenson was touched and delighted. On November 13th, his birthday, the road was presented to him and he gave a party for the donors in the hall of his house. On Thanksgiving Day, November 29th, he gave a party to American and other friends, and appeared in high spirits. He made a speech in which he paid a loving tribute to each member of his family, beginning with his mother, " she who has but lately come back to me from my own native land, she whom with no lessening of affection of others to whom I cling, I love better still than all the world besides." This was the last and one of the gayest of his parties. He was happier than he had been for many months, for he was at last tasting the fruits of all his long years of effort and self-training, of all his laborious devotion to his craft. He was in the full tide of creation and he knew that what he created was good. About the time when the chiefs came to him with the offer of the road, he had really begun *Weir of Hermiston*.

CHAPTER XVII

"WEIR OF HERMISTON"

" *I*N *the wild end of a moorland parish, far out of sight of any house, there stands a cairn among the heather, and a little by the East of it, in the going down of the brae side, a monument with some verses half defaced. It was here that Claverhouse with his own hand shot the Praying Weaver of Balweary, and the chisel of Old Mortality has chinked on that lonely gravestone. Public and domestic history have thus marked with a bloody finger this hollow among the hills; and since the Cameronian gave his life there, two hundred years ago in a glorious folly and without comprehension or regret, the silence of the moss has been broken again by the report of firearms and the cry of the dying.*

"*The Deil's Hag was the old name. But the place is now called Francie's Cairn. For a while it was told that Francie walked. Aggie Hogg met him in the gloaming by the cairn side, and he spoke to her with chattering teeth so that his words were lost. He pursued Rob Todd (if anyone could have believed Robbie) for the space of half a mile with pitiful entreaties. But the age is one of incredulity. These superstitious decorations speedily fell off, and the facts of the story itself, like the bones of a giant buried there and half dug up, survived naked and imperfect in the memory of the scattered neighbours. To this day of winter nights when the sleet is on the window and the cattle are quiet in the byre, there will be told again, amid the silence of the young and the additions and corrections of the old, the tale of the Justice Clerk and of his son, young Hermiston, that vanished from men's knowledge; of the two Kirsties and the four black brothers of*

*the Cauldstaneslap, and of Frank Innes, the 'young fool
advocate' that came into these moorland parts to find his destiny."*

So runs the Preface to Stevenson's last unfinished novel,
Weir of Hermiston. The mark of any genuine work of art
is its inevitability. It grows by its own life. This does not
preclude alteration and reconsideration by the author, who
may see that he has made mistakes in his first attempt to
interpret that life, but it means with a novel that the end
must be implicit in the beginning, the actions must be
implicit in the characters, the style must be the most appropriate for the story, the whole of the story must be implicit
in every part. From the roots in the novelist's heart and mind
the sap must rise strongly through the branches which are
shaped by the best of his skill and experience.

Twice before, in *Treasure Island* and *Kidnapped,* Stevenson
had created stories which had moved by their own impetus,
but both of these were extremely limited in scope. *Weir of
Hermiston* is a novel of far richer content, remarkable not
only for the power and grace of the execution, but for the
brooding sense of destiny which gives it the quality of a
Greek tragedy. From the opening pages when the grim
Adam Weir marries Jeannie Rutherford who " came to her
maturity depressed and, as it were, defaced ; no blood of
life in her, no grasp, no gaiety," from the first word of that
ill-assorted marriage the reader's mind is in tune to the tragic
inheritance of their only son, who was to qualify the father's
brutal vigour with the mother's anaemic spirituality, who
was to hate Adam Weir as Jeannie hated him, and yet to
live under his spell as Jeannie lived. It is the crux of
Stevenson's own life, his dual relationship to his father, with
all the real characters left out, fact transmuted by art into
truth.

In the scheme for the unwritten part of the book, which he disclosed to his stepdaughter who was acting as his amanuensis, Stevenson apparently intended a happy ending overseas for the young lovers, but it is difficult to believe that a novel whose whole tone is tragic could have worked out to such an end. From the beginning Archie Weir seems to be a doomed creature. His mother's early death leaves him alone with his father, a nervous, fastidious boy shut up with a brutal, coarse, stoical figure of crude power, who sums up his utter contempt for all the graces and arts of life in the words " Signor Feedle-eerie." Of course the boy rebels, and, of course, since he is more Jeannie's son than Weir's, his rebellion is abortive. Forbidden the law and scornfully told that he is not man enough to be a soldier, he is sent back to Hermiston to learn to be a laird. There his only real company is the housekeeper, Kirstie, a woman in her own way as powerful and vigorous as the Hanging Judge, against whom she had defended Archie's mother. Now, at fifty, " still a moorland Helen," she falls in love with Archie, a passion half sensual, half maternal, wholly absorbing.

But Kirstie, much as he likes her, is not the destiny waiting for Archie at nineteen. He is intrigued by her stories of her family, " the auld, auld Elliotts, clay cauld Elliotts, dour bold Elliotts of old." Archie plagues Kirstie for stories of the four brothers of the farm at Cauldstaneslap, and learns that they have a young sister, another Christina, now away in Glasgow. Christina comes home, and on a spring morning Archie sees her in church, glowing like a flower in her new town clothes. The two young creatures fall in love at sight. Stevenson, breaking free of his usual inhibitions, describes the girl's ecstasy of chaotic and half-awakened feelings. In the evening she strolls out on to the moors, and instinct which takes her to the Praying Weaver's Stone brings Archie there to meet her at the place where his mother used to pray with him in his childhood, so that from that hour " the two women were enshrined together in his memory."

There is not much more written. Frank Innes, Archie's friend at Edinburgh University, comes to stay with him. He is the bad genius of the book, later, if Stevenson had followed his plan, to seduce Christina and to be murdered by Archie at the Weaver's Stone. Innes discovers Christina, teases Archie about his " highly attractive milkmaid," and asks him what is to be the end of it. Kirstie, who also finds out, puts the same question more seriously, inspired both by concern for Archie and by jealousy of her niece. Archie goes to meet Christina by the Stone, reads her a priggish little lecture, and tells her that they must see less of one another. People have been talking, and " the first thing that we must see to is that there shall be no scandal about for my father's sake." Christina storms at him and then bursts into a passion of tears.

" Archie ran to her. He took the poor child in his arms, and she nestled to his breast as to a mother, clasping him in hands that were strong like vices. He felt her whole body shaken by throes of distress, and had pity upon her beyond speech. Pity and at the same time a bewildered fear of this explosive engine in his arms, whose works he did not understand, and yet had been tampering with . . . in vain he looked back over the interview ; he saw not where he had offended. It seemed unprovoked, a wilful convulsion of brute nature. . . ."

Stevenson dictated these words on the morning of December 3, and then broke off. The mail had come two days ago from England, bringing letters from friends, and he answered some of them. At sunset he came downstairs in high spirits, the afterglow of successful work. Fanny had been sunk all day in a mood of foreboding and depression. He talked to her cheerfully, speaking of a lecture tour that he might make in America, " now that I am so well." They played a game of cards to distract her, but she could not shake off the oppression on her spirits. Stevenson said that he was hungry and asked her to help him make a salad. He went down to the cellar to fetch up a bottle of his special burgundy. They were laying the table on the verandah, and he was still talking gaily when he put both hands to his head and cried out, " What's that ? " He asked, " Do I look strange ? " and fell on his knees. Fanny and his body servant helped him into the hall, where he lay unconscious in a chair. Doctors were called, but nothing could be done : it was a hæmorrhage of the brain. He died at ten minutes past eight.

When the news of his death reached London, his friends mourned not only for the man they had loved and for the books he might have written, but for a keen edge of pleasure in his reception of their own work that they would never find again. Quiller-Couch exclaimed, " Now there is nobody left to write for."

It was his epitaph in the old world. In the country of his adoption they buried him the day after his death on the crest of Mount Vaea. A long procession of Samoans wound past his grave, heaping their ceremonial mats upon it, and one of the chieftains spoke their farewell.

" Tusitala is dead. We were in prison and he cared for us. We were hungry and he fed us. We were sick and he made us well. The day was no longer than his kindness. *Tofa Tusitala*. Sleep, Teller of Tales ! "

CHAPTER XVIII

THE CRAFTSMAN

STEVENSON'S first published work appeared when he was twenty-two. He died in his forty-fifth year, leaving ten complete novels, two of which were written in collaboration with Lloyd Osbourne; five volumes of short stories, one of them written in collaboration with his wife; three volumes of essays; two books on South Sea history; four travel books; four volumes of verse; and a very large number of letters, including the letter-diary written from Samoa to Colvin with the idea of future publication.

The variety of his work was even more astonishing than the quantity. For him every new book was really " a fresh raid on the inarticulate." He did not, as many authors of his quality might have done, resist the temptation to repeat *Treasure Island*. The temptation did not occur to him. For him the interesting book was always the unwritten one.

" Character, character is what he has." So Henry James summed up his work, and went on to say that what makes him rare is the " singular maturity of expression that he has given to young sentiments. The feeling of one's teens and the feeling for happy turns, these in the last analysis are the corresponding halves of his character. . . . Before all things he is a writer with a style."

The man never lost the vision of his childhood. Everything was fresh, new, strange, curious, crammed with possibilities. He saw the world as a boy sees it with himself in the middle of it, as interesting, as crammed with possibilities as any other part of it. His morality, expressed in so many sounding phrases, was the morality that Alison Cunningham had taught him in the nursery. " Be good, don't cry when you fall down, be kind to the others." His philosophy was no philosophy at all. He was never deeply disturbed about the meaning of the universe. He had it taped. It was " a place where any brave man," and he was himself a very brave man, " may make out a life that shall be happy for himself, and so being, beneficent to those about him." Philosophic anxiety did not really touch him. His curiosities were actual, about the beggarman going down the road, the history of an old inn, the flavour of a new wine, the manners and customs of South Sea Islanders. " He was reconciled to life," Henry James went on to say, " because it is the widest field that we know of for odd doings." There is no thought in his philosophy, it is the expression of a rooted emotional faith that was the colour of his blood and the marrow of his bones, the faith that life was worth living for its own sake.

This belief gave an immense zest to his writing, and to his company, but the fact that in the heart of his life he never questioned it kept him always like Will o' the Mill on the threshold of experience. He is the writer of the threshold. His particular contribution is to express that early morning spirit of youth and expectancy which shrinks with most men into a vestigial memory, but which remained the essence of his nature. A writer gains by his losses. It is easy to suggest that Stevenson's growth was fundamentally retarded by the too great strain of his double feeling for his father, by the cramping demands that his Covenanting childhood made on the sensitive spirit of the embryo artist, by the fact that being often lonely, ill and unhappy as a child, he had to go under or clutch at fantasy and optimism. Admitting that all these narrowed his development as a man and therefore as a writer, it must also be admitted that they were the things that helped to form the individual man and writer, Robert Louis Stevenson.

By the odd contradiction that Henry James noted, the writer was from the first astonishingly mature. His twenty-two-year-old essays in the *Cornhill* and other periodicals at once struck the discerning critics as being the work of " a new artist of great promise," not for what he said, but for the distinctive way in which he said it. The quality of his prose was "personal, expressive, renewed at every attempt." At its best, in *Treasure Island*, in the " Flight through the Heather " chapters in *Kidnapped*, in the " Duel " scene in *The Master of Ballantrae*, in many of his short stories, and most of all in *Weir of Hermiston*, it was beautiful, Greek in its freshness, economy and directness. At its worst, as in parts of *Prince Otto*, and in some of the more portentous essays, it was mannered, self-conscious and jaunty. It was never flabby, stale or careless. He never used a word because it happened to be the next word on the shelf in the store cupboard. He spared no pains. " I live," he once wrote to Colvin, "for my dexterities. Even my clumsinesses are my joy, my woodcuts, my stumbling on the pipe . . . even weeding."

Writing was the first of his dexterities. As a boy he had lived with words. Throughout his life he gave to the nice use of words an unremitting energy and a loving devotion. This is his honourable place in English Letters, his value to readers with an ear and especially to other writers. He was before all things a craftsman.

ROBERT LOUIS STEVENSON

1850. Born November 13.

1873. Meeting with Sidney Colvin.   Publication of first essay.

1877. First short story published.

1878. First book published (*Inland Voyage*).

1879. First journey to America.

1880. Marriage to Fanny Van de Grift Osbourne.

1883. *Treasure Island* published.

1886. *Dr. Jekyll and Mr. Hyde* published.

1887. Second journey to America.

1888. Voyage to South Seas.

1890. Settled at Samoa.

1894. Died December 3.

WORKS

NOVELS

Treasure Island (1883), *Prince Otto* (1885), *Dr. Jekyll and Mr. Hyde* (1886), *Kidnapped* (1886), *The Black Arrow* (1888), *The Wrong Box* (1889) [with LLOYD OSBOURNE], *The Master of Ballantrae* (1889), *The Wrecker* (1892) [with LLOYD OSBOURNE], *Catriona* (1893), *The Ebb Tide* (1894), *St. Ives* (unfinished) (1897), *Weir of Hermiston* (unfinished) (1896).

BOOKS OF TRAVEL

An Inland Voyage (1878), *Travels with a Donkey in the Cevennes* (1879), *The Silverado Squatters* (1883), *Across the Plains* (at first called *The Amateur Emigrant*) (1892).

POEMS

A Child's Garden of Verses (1885), *Underwoods* (1887), *Ballads* (1890), *Songs of Travel and Other Verses* (1896).

SHORT STORIES

> *New Arabian Nights* (1882), *More New Arabian Nights, The Dynamiter* (1885) [with FANNY OSBOURNE], *The Merry Men and Other Tales and Fables* (1887), *Island Nights' Entertainments* (1893).

ESSAYS

> *Virginibus Puerisque and Other Papers* (1881), *Edinburgh: Picturesque Notes* (1879), *Familiar Studies of Men and Books* (1882), *Memories and Portraits* (1887).

MISCELLANEOUS

> *Memoir of Fleeming Jenkin* (1887), *A Footnote to History, Eight Years of Trouble in Samoa* (1892), *Father Damien, An Open Letter to the Reverend Dr. Hyde of Honolulu* (1890), *Letters*.

SOME BOOKS OF REFERENCE

Stevenson's own letters and autobiographical essays.

Prefaces to Stevenson's Works. By FANNY OSBOURNE and LLOYD OSBOURNE.

Prefaces to the Letters. By SIDNEY COLVIN.

" R.L.S." in *Partial Portraits*. By HENRY JAMES.

Life of Stevenson. By GRAHAM BALFOUR.

Robert Louis Stevenson, Man and Writer. By J. A. STEUART.

Robert Louis Stevenson, A Critical Study. By FRANK SWINNERTON.

Life of Stevenson. By ROSALINE MASSON.

R. L. Stevenson. By JANET ADAM SMITH.

Robert Louis Stevenson in the " English Men of Letters " Series. By SYEPHEN GWYNN.

INDEX